Social Economy in the Basque Country

Current Research Series No. 12

Social Economy
in the
Basque Country

EDITED BY AITOR BENGOETXEA ALKORTA

Center for Basque Studies
University of Nevada, Reno

This book was published with generous financial support of the Basque government.

Current Research Series No. 12
Center for Basque Studies
University of Nevada, Reno
Reno, Nevada 89557
http://basque.unr.edu

Library of Congress Cataloging-in-Publication Data

Bengoetxea Alkorta, Aitor, editor.
Title: Social economy / edited by Aitor Bengoetxea Alkorta.
Description: Reno, Nevada : Center for Basque Studies,
University of Nevada
Reno, [2018] | Series: Current research series ; No. 12
Includes bibliographical references.
Identifiers: LCCN 2018041839 | ISBN 9781935709961 (pbk.)
Subjects: LCSH: País Vasco (Spain)--Economic conditions.
Pays Basque
(France)--Economic conditions.
País Vasco (Spain)--Social conditions.
Pays Basque (France)--Social conditions.

Classification:

LCC HC387.P28 S63 2018
DDC 306.30946/6--dc23

Contents

Introduction

AITOR BENGOETXEA ALKORTA

In the social economy area and, more concretely, in the cooperative field, the Basque Country has, no doubt unintentionally, become a worldwide benchmark. The dynamism that energizes Basque social initiatives has resulted in outstanding examples of good practices in which firms' priorities are guided by social aims that respond to social needs, steering clear of the commercial profit mechanisms that are the main global driver of private economic initiative.

The work we present here originated in the "Social Economy Conference" held on June 28, 2017, in Donostia-San Sebastián, under the heading "The Reality of the Social Economy in the Euroregion: A Cross-border Perspective." The conference was organized by the GEZKI Institute (Gizarte Ekonomia eta Zuzenbide Kooperatiboaren Institutua, Institute of Cooperative Law and Social Economy), at the University of the Basque Country. This academic event received funding and collaboration from the Basque government, the government de Navarre, and the Center for Basque Studies at the University of Nevada, Reno. The conference was devoted to analyzing the social economy in the different Basque territories (the Basque Autonomous Community, the Autonomous Community of Navarre, and the Northern Basque Country). Representatives of both governments gave papers, setting out the social economy promotion policies developed by their respective institutions.

This book contains nine studies covering a variety of aspects of the Basque social economy.

The work begins with a general reflection on the concept of the social economy by Enekoitz Etxezarreta and Eusebio Lasa. They make the point that, although the social economy is a well-established concept, it receives a different level of institutional recognition according to the country one is referring to, as emerging concepts very close to that of the social economy have also appeared, outstripping it in popularity. In this regard, they emphasize that the concept of the solidarity economy makes innovative proposals, perceiving that the idea of the social economy can contribute significantly to the development of a more human social model, so long as it exploits all the potential for transformation that it contains.

Continuing with this line of conceptual analysis, Igone Altzelai brings to the collection a study of the third social sector in Euskadi (the Basque Country), concerning those who are vulnerable and at risk of social exclusion. She analyzes the recently passed Law 6/2016, of May 12, on the Third Social Sector, placing it within the context of Spanish and European regulations in this area. Given the wide variety of rules, bodies, and institutions involved, the author asks whether third social sector organizations, social initiative organizations, third social action sector entities, social economy entities, and social enterprises are equivalent legal categories or not, and deliberates about the relation that exists among them. And that question leads her in turn to another, preliminary line of inquiry, regarding the interrelation between the social economy and the third sector. This study, then, sets out to develop a valid approach armed with efficient criteria for interpretation to verify whether a specific entity does or does not belong to the area of the social economy or to that of the third sector.

Aitor Bengoetxea, meanwhile, provides an overview of the social economy in the Basque Country, in accordance with the various concurrent legal spaces in Europe, France, Spain, and the Basque Country. He analyzes the regulatory powers that the different Basque public authorities possess in the matter. The subject of analysis is the social economy in general, as well as the law governing each of the entities that comprise it: cooperatives; mutual and friendly societies; associations; foundations; worker-owned companies; insertion companies; special employment centers; agricultural processing companies; and fishermen's guilds. His purpose is to lay out the legal framework of the social economy and of its entities within the Basque Country, identifying the regulatory channel that must be followed by social economy initiatives developed in our territory.

Aratz Soto and Ane Etxebarria furnish a precise picture of the current reality of the social economy sector in the Autonomous Community of Euskadi, as well as of its recent development at the turn of this century, presenting and analyzing socioeconomic data for the sector and the legislation governing it. For their task, they base their analysis on work that both researchers have been engaged in at the Basque Social Economy Observatory, housed in the GEZKI Institute. They analyze the evolution and situation of the most significant social economy families in Euskadi. Their chapter closes with some final remarks on the present and future of the social economy in the three Basque provinces of Araba, Bizkaia, and Gipuzkoa.

Mikel Irujo's contribution studies the promotion of the social economy offered by the bodies of the European Union, as well as a specific, detailed view of the Autonomous Community of Navarre. He underlines the importance of the Comprehensive Social Economy Plan of Navarre for the period comprising 2017–2020 as the best example of policies promoting the social economy in this territory.

Jon Morandeira and Ane Etxebarria then offer a theoretical approach to the classification of public promotion policies dealing with the social economy in Europe. They examine the theoretical framework for these public policies aimed at promoting, divulging, and boosting the social economy, differentiating between policies that impact on the structure of the sector, supporting the creation and development of entities, and employment policies that directly affect employment *in* those entities.

The three last sections of the book concentrate on cooperativism, adopting diverse perspectives to do so.

Xabier Itçaina studies associated work cooperatives in the Northern Basque Country (French Basque Country), applying an interdisciplinary perspective that straddles political sociology and economic sociology. He explores the influence of territorial cultures and identities in local development policy, focusing on associated work cooperatives, and looking at interactions between this organizational model and sociopolitical and economic dynamics. The author sets out to unravel the complete linkage between the cultural, economic, and sociopolitical factors that affect this territory. Using qualitative research on the associated work cooperatives of the French Basque Country he tries to get to the heart of the puzzle.

Ignacio Bretos and Anjel Errasti take us onto thorny ground indeed, covering the globalization of the cooperative movement, and the viability of cooperatives and their values and hallmarks within a capitalist environment. Over the last decades, marked by the intensification of the process of neoliberal globalization, a debate has emerged once again around the viability of cooperatives under the new conditions imposed by globalization and their capacity for retaining their cooperative practices and values while staying competitive in the markets and proving to be efficient in economic-business terms. The authors analyze the main references in the academic literature in this regard, in which they distinguish two trends of thought. On one hand, there is the pessimistic and strongly predominant "theory of degeneration," which holds that the cooperative movement is sinking into conventional forms of entrepreneurship under organizational models and priorities resembling those of capitalist firms. On the other, there is the "theory of regeneration," an idea that suggests that cooperatives can manage to hold onto their original nature in the long term, and that this degeneration may constitute a temporary stage. Beyond strictly academic sources, their study is rooted in recent empirical works on the Mondragon Group, and in qualitative research conducted by the authors in recent years in some of the most important multinational cooperatives in the group, taking in Fagor Ederlan, Maier, and Fagor Electrodomésticos, and utilizing primary (interviews) and secondary data (internal documentation furnished by the Mondragon Group).

The book culminates with the contribution of Aitziber Etxezarreta, Santiago Merino, Gala Cano, and Artitzar Erauskin, who approach the subject of housing cooperatives. They center on the tenant housing cooperative model, which seems to be gaining ground and influence as a specific formula within the Basque government's public housing policy framework.

I should like to conclude by acknowledging the authors for all their contributions to the present work. For their input and support I must also sincerely thank Jokin Díaz (Director of the Social Economy for the Basque government), Mikel Irujo (Delegate of the Government of Navarre in Brussels), and Xabier Irujo (Director of the Center for Basque Studies at the University of Nevada, Reno), first of all for making possible the Conference on the Social Economy held in Donostia-San Sebastián on June 28 2017, and secondly for their good offices in which production and publication of this collection are concerned.

I am, inevitably, greatly satisfied to see this book come into being as a modest extension of knowledge and reflection on the rich and complex dynamic that informs the Basque social economy.

1

The Social Economy Concept: Process of Consolidation and Future Challenges

Enekoitz Etxezarreta and Eusebio Lasa

Both at the European level and in our own context, the social economy is a fully consolidated concept whose strength lies in the identification of certain legal entities as a means of delimiting the sector. Each country, however, has a different level of institutional recognition for the social economy, and indeed emergent concepts whose approach is not so dissimilar are coming into being and outstripping it in popularity. The social economy shows some limitations when it comes to incorporating more political, transformative proposals within its form of operating. The solidarity economy makes innovative proposals in this regard, in considering that the social economy can contribute significantly to the development of a more human social model, so long as it exploits all the potential for transformation that it contains.

Consolidation Process of the Concept: A European View

The social economy concept today enjoys important legal and political recognition in different European countries. For a better understanding of the contents that tend to be associated with it we must firstly provide a brief interpretation of the main landmarks in its historical development.

The social economy arrived on the scene as a socioeconomic reality in the mid-nineteenth century, due to the emergence of the cooperative phenomenon, and received new endorsement at the end of the twentieth century with the arrival of the "new" social economy. At these two historical points, the conceptual development of the social economy was established as a consequence of the interaction of three social agents (Etxezarreta 2014): first, the economic agents in the sector, expressed through various networks and entities, made their claim as realities that differed from other economic agents; once the sector was introduced in society in a unified manner, the academy began to consider it as a specific object of study; and, eventually, the public decision-makers sought to profile, devise, and adopt promotional measures for the sector.

From an Economic Reality to an Object of Study and Recognition in Europe

The social economy emerged as a response to nineteenth-century industrial capitalist development through experiences of self-management linked with the cooperative movement. The first "social economists" began to theorize about the cooperative undertakings promoted principally by activists such as Robert Owen and Charles Fourier, whose roots lay in utopian socialism. Many of the cooperative principles, which were definitively established much later in the 1995 declaration of the ICA (International Co-operative Alliance), were those laid down in what was regarded as the pioneer experience in

Rochdale, England, in 1844, encompassing free membership, democratic management, economic participation, education, and so on.

The term social economy was established for the first time to denominate such experiences that stood apart from other economic realities because of their moralizing mission (which impinged on the behavior of individuals) and also because they represented more efficient human forms of organization (Monzón 2003; Chaves 1997).

The last quarter of the twentieth century, as Europe suffered from an industrial downturn and an accompanying crisis of its welfare states, witnessed a renewed emergence of social economy entities, although this time there were more links among the various agents that made up the sector. Both in France and in Belgium, cooperatives, friendly societies, and associations began to organize jointly through different councils and commissions. In 1980 in France, the National Liaison Committee for Mutual, Cooperative, and Associative Activities (Comité national de liaison des activités mutualistes coopératives et associatives, CNLAMCA) published a charter of principles, which established for the first time in Europe a list of seven principles shared by these entities: the primacy of the individual; voluntary membership; democratic control; a combination of mutual and general interest; solidarity; management autonomy; and profit sharing policies. The most recent Europe-wide declaration of principles occurred in 2002 in the shape of *Social Economy Europe,* in which the principles listed above[1] were ratified (with some nuances).

The emergence of the first research centers to specialize in the analysis of this object of study occurred around the same time: CIRIEC-International (Centre International de Recherches et d'Information sur l'Economie Publique, Sociale et Coopérative,

---

1 In this case the principles agreed were the following: The primacy of the individual and the social objective over capital; voluntary and open membership; democratic control by the membership (this does not concern foundations as they have no members); the combination of the interests of members/ users and/or the general interest; the defense and application of the principle of solidarity and responsibility; autonomous management and independence from public authorities; and, finally, most of the surpluses are used in pursuit of sustainable development objectives, services of interest to members, or the general interest.

International Centre of Research and Information on the Public, Social and Cooperative Economy) was one of them. This network of university researchers would make major contributions in consolidating this concept, for when the theoretical specificities of these experiences were being systematized, they also conducted statistical measurement studies in the sector in accordance with the European national accounting systems.

An important step forward was taken in this regard with the publication of the "Satellite Accounts of Companies in the Social Economy" (Barea and Monzón 1995, 2007; Monzón 2010), because it lays down a suitable methodology of measurement in the sector for national accounting systems. Based on this contribution, the CIRIEC[2] constructed a proposal for defining the social economy.

When the sector had defined itself in a collective sense and suitable methodologies of measurement had been devised, the decision-makers set out to strengthen the sector through various kinds of public policies. In Europe, on the heels of the pioneering Social Economy Law passed in Spain in 2011, different national laws were endorsed (in Portugal, France, Belgium, Greece, and Romania) that were, basically, aimed at endowing the sector with legal certainty and reinforcing its public functioning through concrete procedures.

The social economy also receives growing institutional recognition within the European Union, and not just among the member states. As José Luis Monzón (2016) rightly contends, under the presidency of Jaques Delors (1985–95) definitive impetus was given to the cooperative approach, and thanks to this momentum two goals were accomplished that have clearly proved to be of great importance for the sector: The setting up of the European Parliament's Social Economy Intergroup, through which a whole range of rulings and

---

2 Through this methodology the social economy was divided into two subsectors, the market and the nonmarket, and this methodology is valid for achieving reliable statistics for economic activities in line with the national accounts system. The European Commission has now established a guideline entitled *Manual for Drawing up the Satellite Accounts of Companies in the Social Economy (Co-operatives and Mutual Societies)*, which contains the satellite accounts of cooperatives and mutual societies based on accounts designed in Spain, in Belgium, and in Macedonia-Serbia in 2011.

action plans have been promoted since 1990; and the creation of the *Social Economy Europe* initiative within the European Commission, in which European cooperatives, friendly societies, associations, and foundations are represented.

Recent Developments in the Basque Country, Spain, and France

The review carried out by José Luis Monzón (2016) finds that the conceptual development in Spain and in the Southern Basque Country has followed a similar course.

The sector in Spain began to be organized in the 1980s through the creation of COCETA[3] (Confederación Española de Cooperativas de Trabajo Asociado, Spanish Confederation of Associated Work Cooperatives) and CONFESAL[4] (Confederación Empresarial de Sociedades Laborales de España, Confederation of Spanish Labor Companies). The main body representing the cooperative sector today is CEPES-Spain (Confederación Empresarial Española de la Economía Social· Spanish Business Confederation of the Social Economy),[5] which has been operating since 1992. As far as institutional recognition goes, the creation in 1990 of the INFES (Instituto Nacional de Fomento de la Economía Social, National Institute for the Promotion of the Social Economy) set a first milestone on a path that led to the passing of Law 5/2011 on the Social Economy. The impact of this law has been widely studied (Pérez de Uralde 2014; Etxezarreta and Morandeira 2012; Fajardo 2012;), although its principal contribution can be summed up in two core aspects: it has helped to make the sector visible; and it has established the legal framework for adopting measures for promoting the sector, although many argue that there has been zero regulatory development since the law was passed.

---

3 http://www.coceta.coop/.
4 https://www.confesal.org/WEB/index.php.
5 http://www.cepes.es/.

In the Basque Country, the social economy has been somewhat of a reference point due to the cooperative movement organized around the Mondragón Group. This experience has been studied profusely by researchers at an international level yet, paradoxical though it might seem, it has scarcely had any presence in the study plans and curricular offerings of Basque universities.

Beyond the Mondragón Group, the Basque social economy enjoys a strong organization through entities representing each of the families. In the Autonomous Community of the Basque Country (ACBC), the four large families of the Basque social economy are: the Cooperative Confederation (KONFEKOOP);[6] the Association of Labor Companies in the Basque Country (Sociedades Laborales de Euskadi-Euskadiko Lan Sozietateak, ASLE;[7] the Association of Sheltered Workshops in the Basque Country (Euskal Herriko Lan Babestuaren Elkartea, EHLABE);[8] and the Association of Social Integration Enterprises in the Basque Country (GIZATEA).[9] Recently, the Basque Social Economy Network (Euskal Gizarte Ekonomiaren Sarea-Red Vasca de Economía Social, EGES)[10] was created, which incorporates all the families mentioned; including the Alternative Solidarity Economy Network of the Basque Country (Red de Economía Alternativa y Solidaria, REAS-Euskadi).[11]

In the Autonomous Community of Navarre, the representative entities are organized around the Social Economy Business Confederation of Navarre (Confederación Empresarial de Economía Social de Navarra, CEPES-Navarra):[12] the Association of Social Economy Enterprises of Navarre (Asociación Navarra de Empresas Laborales, ANEL);[13] the Union of Agricultural Cooperatives of Navarre (Unión de Cooperativas Agrarias de Navarra, UCAN);[14] the Navarrese Association of Social and Labor Insertion Centers

6 https://www.konfekoop.coop/?idioma=es.
7 http://asle.es/.
8 http://www.ehlabe.org/.
9 http://www.gizatea.net/.
10 https://www.eges.eus/es-eges.
11 https://www.economiasolidaria.org/reas-euskadi.
12 http://www.cepesnavarra.org/.
13 *http://www.anel.es/*.
14 http://ucan.es/.

(Centros de Inserción Sociolaboral, CIS);[15] and the Alternative Solidarity Economy Network of Navarre (REAS-Navarra).[16]

Public policies aimed at stimulating the sector in the ACBC are mainly channeled through the Social Economy Office, which is part of the Department of Work and Justice in the Basque government, although there are, in addition, different offices of a more sectoral kind that service various agents in the sector (associations, foundations, agricultural companies, fishermen's guilds, and so on). Apart from these bodies, the Basque Supreme Council of Cooperatives (Consejo Superior de Cooperativas de Euskadi-Euskadiko Kooperatiben Goren-Kontseilua)[17] serves as the main meeting space for guaranteeing the promotion and dissemination of cooperatives, and it acts as an advisor to the Basque public administrations on cooperative matters. In the Autonomous Community of Navarre, public policies are designed through the Department of Economic Development, in which the Social Economy Plan for 2017–2020 has just been endorsed, thanks to the collaboration of the main organizations in the sector.

Lastly, at the university level, there are three institutes specializing in the field of the social economy: GEZKI;[18] Lanki;[19] and IEC;[20] which are, respectively, attached to the University of the Basque Country (UPV/EHU), Mondragon University, and the University of Deusto. And while this subject is still very limited at the undergraduate degree level, there are more specialized graduate courses on offer.[21]

In France, in Xabier Itçaina's view (2017), the social economy reached a high point thanks to the passing of the 2014 Law on the Social and Solidarity Economy, which follows the line taken by the

---

15 http://www.centrosdeinsercion.org/centrosdeinsercion/Centros_de_Insercion_Navarra.html.
16 http://www.economiasolidaria.org/reasnavarra.
17 http://www.csce-ekgk.coop/es/.
18 http://www.gezki.eus.
19 http://www.mondragon.edu/eu/huhezi/ikerketa/ikerketa-taldeak/lanki.
20http://derecho.deusto.es/cs/Satellite/derecho/es/instituto-de-estudios-cooperativos-0.
21 https://www.ehu.eus/es/web/economiasocialysolidaria/aurkezpena.

Spanish and Portuguese laws. This legislation lends new endorsement to this sector, which had already been acknowledged to some extent since the early 1980s owing to the Charter of Principles established by the CNLAMCA.

Coming closer to home now and focusing on the Northern Basque Country, Itçaina (2017) points out that in the 1970s, due to campaigning by the Basque nationalist movement, different local development experiences were initiated. The Mondragón cooperatives, in turn, provided assistance and advice at close quarters in the creation of new cooperatives in the Northern Basque Country. Associated work cooperatives began to link together around the Partzuer association[22] in 1974. Hemen-Herrikoa[23] was established in 1979–1980 as a venture capital tool. At the same time, in the rural economy other organizations were established. These included the farmers' union, ELB (Euskal Herriko Laborarien Batasuna, Union of Basque Farmworkers);[24] and the Arrapitz Federation,[25] devoted to the promotion of rural development. These movements continued to evolve until a new leap was taken in 2000, when they were joined by new initiatives associated with consumption and exchange. The increasing environmental awareness crystallized in proximity initiatives. One example of this was the creation in 2012 of the Eusko, an alternative social currency to the Euro. This new wave in the social economy also strengthened ties with projects on the other side of the border, in areas such as organic farming, the Basque language, culture, communication, and the media. Interestingly, many of these undertakings became integrated within the Pôle Territorial de Coopération Économique (Territorial Center for Economic Cooperation, PTCE),[26] located in Tarnos, in South Aquitaine.

---

22 http://www.euskonews.com/0664zbk/elkar_eu.html.
23 http://hemen-herrikoa.org/.
24 http://www.euskonews.com/0492zbk/ebooks49204eu.html.
25 http://www.argia.eus/argia-astekaria/1760/arrapitz-federazioa.
26https://www.economie.gouv.fr/files/files/PDF/20150421_dossier_de_
   presse_ptce.pdf.

Lack of Agreement at the European Level: The Social Economy and Related Concepts

From what has been analyzed so far one may deduce that the social economy concept is broadly shared at the European level due to the myriad representative bodies, institutional rulings, studies undertaken, and regulatory developments we have pointed to. It is also true, however, that there is uneven recognition across Europe, given that there are other concepts that are very close to the social economy that compete with one other to strengthen their position as the best accepted options.

Two concepts, according to José Luis Monzón and Rafael Chaves (2017), have traditionally emerged in proximity to that of the social economy: nonprofit organizations and the idea of the solidarity economy. In recent years, still another set of emerging proposals has come into play: social enterprise, the collaborative economy, the economy for the common good, the circular economy, and corporate social responsibility. A detailed study of the meaning of each of these concepts and the distinctions between them are beyond the reach of this work.[27] We have instead chosen here to mention only two notions that we deem to be regarded as the most significant in international comparative studies: these are the third sector and the social economy.

Comparative Studies at the European Level

In our understanding, among recent works two comparative international studies that have set out to analyze the degree of existing conceptual consensus at a European level stand out. Both of them are rigorous and utilize a similar methodological framework: the first is a study coordinated by José Luis Monzón and Rafael Chaves (2017), collected in the work entitled *Recent Evolutions of the Social Economy in the European Union*; and the second is directed by Lester

---

27 To consult comparative studies, see: Monzón and Rafael Chaves (2012, 2017,); Pérez de Mendiguren, Etxezarreta, and Guridi (2009); and Monzón (2006).

Salamon and S. Wojciech Kolokowsky (2014), published under the title *The Third Sector in Europe: Towards a Consensus Conceptualization.*

While the former adopts the theoretical approach of the social economy, the second contribution clearly bears the seal of the nonprofit organizations school. However, since in Europe (with the exception of the English-speaking countries) the term "nonprofit" is not so typical, they employ the "third center" concept as a consensus proposal. In both studies we observe that the European countries have several ways of designating this sector. We will look at each in turn.

As we see in the table below, Monzón and Chaves (2017) establish three groups of countries in terms of the degree to which the social economy concept is accepted: countries in which it is most acknowledged, such as Spain, France, Portugal, Belgium, and Luxemburg; a more heterogeneous group in which there is an average level of acceptance, including Italy, Greece, Cyprus, Finland, Sweden, Denmark, and others; and countries in which there is least recognition, including Austria, the Czech Republic, Germany, Estonia, Latvia, and Lithuania.

The authors conclude that the most widespread concepts resembling the social economy are the notions of nonprofit organizations, social enterprise, and the third sector, while those of the solidarity economy and the economy for the common good receive far less support. If we classify this by zones, the Nordic countries are most inclined to employ the term "social enterprise," while in the Eastern European countries "nonprofit organizations" and "voluntary sector" are most commonly used.

Country	Code	By public authorities	By social economy companies and federations	By the academic/scientific world
AUSTRIA	AT	*	**	**
BELGIUM	BE	***	***	**
BULGARIA	BG	**	**	**
CROATIA	HR	*	**	*
CYPRUS	CY	**	**	**
CZECH REPUBLIC	CZ	*	**	**
DENMARK	DK	**	**	**
ESTONIA	EE	**	**	*
FINLAND	FI	**	**	**
FRANCE	FR	***	***	**
GERMANY	DE	*	**	**
GREECE	EL	**	**	***
HUNGARY	HU	**	**	**
IRELAND	IE	**	***	**
ITALY	IT	**	**	**
LATVIA	LV	*	**	**
LITHUANIA	LT	**	**	*
LUXEMBOURG	LU	***	***	**
MALTA	MT	**	*	**
NETHERLANDS	NL	*	*	*
POLAND	PL	**	***	**
PORTUGAL	PT	***	***	**
ROMANIA	RO	**	**	**
SLOVAKIA	SK	*	*	**
SLOVENIA	SI	**	***	**
SPAIN	ES	***	***	***
SWEDEN	SE	**	**	**
UNITED KINGDOM	UK	**	**	**

* Little recognition / ** Moderate recognition / *** High recognition

Table 2.1. Degree of recognition of the Social
Economy in the European Union.
Source: José Luis Monzón and Rafael Chaves, 2017: 35

Salamon and Kolokowsky (2014) conclude that a great variety of concepts are used in Europe to denote the third sector or entities that represent that space (namely, that which is neither state-public or commercial-profit). In their opinion the social economy concerns a specific type of entity, while the third sector, by contrast, is used to designate a variety of far more diverse entities. Consequently, the way this third sector is characterized depends on the nature of the entities in each country.

According to this study, the most commonly used term in the English-speaking countries is "public charities"; in the Central European countries, "nonprofit organizations" and "civil society"; and in Southern Europe, the "social economy." In Scandinavia and in the Eastern European countries no single notion reaches a reasonable degree of consensus, so a very varied collection of terms is in use.

The Search for Principles of Consensus

From a comparative analysis of the results at the international level we can draw a first conclusion: one of the principal weaknesses of the social economy concept is its classification into legal entities or organizations by type. We must bear in mind that each country possesses different legislation and legal entities are, consequently, different. Thus, while cooperatives are very frequent in countries with a French-speaking tradition, they are practically banned in the post-Soviet world. Likewise, although in English-speaking countries the charity as a formula is deeply rooted, this model is not totally standardized in many countries and examples of a similar nature would have to be sought ("associations" or "civil society organizations"). This lack of standardization of the legal status leads us, for the purposes of proposing a more useful and internationally understandable concept, to classify the sector in terms of more general principles.

Salamon and Kolokowsky (2014) consider the third sector concept to be the most appropriate consensus designation for use in Europe. According to both authors, although there are differences as to the kind of organizations that may fit within this concept, a consensus has been reached for defining the three basic principles of the third sector in Europe: they are collective and individual nonprofit governance initiatives; the aim is to create something useful for third parties and collectives; and work is conducted through voluntary (and never compulsory) activities.

Under these principles, the following would fall within this concept: 1. All nonprofit organizations;[28] 2. cooperatives and friendly societies linked to the social economy, so long as they guarantee "a limited distribution of the profits," thereby remaining at a remove from "for-profit" business models; 3. social enterprises, provided that they guarantee "a limited distribution of the profits," thereby remaining at a remove from "for-profit" business models; and 4. beyond the institutions, individual initiatives based on voluntary work would also be taken into account, as this notion in some countries is closely related to the participation of civil society and voluntary service.

As against the third sector concept, which comes very close to the perspective of nonprofit organizations, Monzón and Chaves (2017) define the social economy concept by establishing three differentiating features:

- The criterion of nonprofit: this standard would not be a general requirement within the social economy because firms that distribute the profits are the most representative organizations in this collective (cooperatives and friendly societies).

- The criterion of democracy: the social economy concept sets this standard as the main differentiating feature, turning away organizations that do not guarantee democratic practice.

- The criterion of serving people: while the social economy specifically stipulates that its activity must be addressed toward the benefit of individuals or of other

---

28 Defined in the United Nations *Handbook on Nonprofit Institutions in the System of National Account* as NPIs, or nonprofit institutions.

social economy organizations, the third sector defines this in a much more heterogeneous way, because nonprofit organizations can be created for the benefit of the organizations that control or finance them.

To sum up, in Europe there has been a rapprochement among the concepts that compete with the social economy, and the differentiating features are as follows: the third sector designation rebuffs market agents and welcomes voluntary individuals; the social economy, while it does not stand in the way of market agents, is committed to performing collective democratic activity at the service of people.

Challenges for the Future: Innovative Proposals

We can draw a dual conclusion from the preceding two sections. Over the last forty years the social economy has been strengthened as a consequence of identifying the sector with concrete legal entities. Such a definition of the sector favors its visibility, through measurement of the statistical data (adapted to standards of national accounting) and by better limiting the target of public policies for the sector's development.

Be that as it may, the very choice that benefitted its empowerment brought with it other more negative consequences, exposing the concept's limits: standardization at an international level becomes complicated, as the legal entities and their corresponding regulations vary depending on the country in question. But, from our point of view, over and above these issues of standardization there are two core problems that limit the potential of the social economy:

- If the concept ignores the real practice of the social economy, just taking a specific legal form of the concept does not always guarantee that the entity's practice will be grounded in democracy and in solidarity. Very frequently we witness a contradiction between rhetoric and practice (Pérez de Mendiguren and Etxezarreta 2015b).

- Beyond the legal entities associated with the social economy, the concept also forgets other transformative democratic practices, especially those that stem from the field of the solidarity economy (Pérez de Mendiguren and Etxezarreta 2015)

The solidarity economy proposal endorses these two latter criticisms of the social economy and, at the same time, suggests going beyond some of its limits. As we will see below, this new term, solidarity economy, offers innovative and refreshing elements to the concept of the social economy.

A Proposal to Renovate the Solidarity Economy

Jean Louis Laville (2013) proposes that the solidarity economy be endorsed as a way of overcoming the contradictions of the social economy. For Laville (2013), the social economy has moved away from its own logic and has drawn increasingly closer to the dominant logics of the market and the state.

The processes of isomorphism that the term has undergone are the result of a lack of critical spirit, for it puts forward no reflections upon the economy as a whole or upon the way in which the social economy acts in the market. Today the prime objective of the social economy is to be competitive in the market, pushing into the background objectives of a social nature. From the institutionalist viewpoint (Brunsson 1989; Meyer and Rowan 1977), these processes have also been regarded as a "distortion" between theory and practice. From this perspective, Laville (2013) contends that social economy agents squander its very capacity for transformation.

The solidarity economy proposal, in consequence, aims to go beyond certain limits imposed by the traditional interpretation of the social economy, taking into consideration other business realities (insertion companies, fair trade, or ethical financing, for example) and proposing at the same time other analytical tools that neoclassical theory does not offer, theorizing and showing another way of understanding and seeing the economy.

Thus, this proposal aims to broaden the social economy concept, in which at least three aspects are concerned (Pérez de Mendiguren and Etxezarreta 2015): in the organizational field, embracing various dynamics that are not taken up by the social economy (non-monetary ones, for instance); in the policy field, proposing a deepening of the political function of the social economy; and in the theoretical field, building a new theoretical corpus to stand up against hegemonic economic theories.

Starting at the end, the solidarity economy seeks to revise the economy as a scholarly discipline, calling into question two of the basic columns of the neoclassical school. One is the paradigm of *homo economicus* according to which people, individually and collectively, act in their economic activity in a rational, selfish, competitive, and utilitarian manner. The other is the conception that the economy is a formal, free, isolated science (Coraggio 2009, 2011):[29] the solidarity economy casts doubts on both these positions.

For the theoreticians of the solidarity economy, neoclassical theory imposes clear limits on the way the economy is understood, especially where three aspects are concerned: the economic field is isolated from other social spaces, and is basically equal to the market; at the same time, the market is understood as a self-regulated space and there is, in consequence, no need for other social institutions to intervene to regulate it; and, lastly, the modern firm is placed on the same level as the capitalist firm, omitting from any analysis all non-capitalist institutions (Laville 2004).

One can overcome these limits, imposed by the neoclassical theoretical framework, by incorporating two key contributions of the alternative model constructed by anthropologist and economist Karl Polanyi (2007). First, as opposed to the formalist point of view fueled by the present conventional economy, we are urged

---

29 For the neoclassical approach, the economy is understood as a science apart from the rest of the social and the natural sciences, in isolation, where its fundamental interest is to maximize individual interests in self-regulated markets. This interpretation lies beyond any ethical consideration, since it does not call into question, among other aspects, either the preferences of individual people or the legitimacy of the origin of the returns received by those people.

to apply the substantive approach to the economy. Second, and linked to the previous idea, there is recognition of the plurality of economic principles, bringing to the fore, in economic as well as market relations, other regulatory norms and symbolic values. In tangible terms, we are talking of three different logics or "principles of integration": these are exchange, redistribution, and reciprocity, and different economic spaces fall into place where each of the previous logics is predominant: the market economy, the state, and community space, among others.

This epistemological proposal, as well as adding stringency to academic research, has clear political consequences, since the fact that an activity is social demands a resocialization and a repoliticization of the economy. In the same line of reasoning, the solidarity economy is bound to be economic (from a plural perspective of the economy), but it cannot be apolitical or politically uncritical (Dacheux and Goujon 2011). Some authors, however, argue that sufficient unity and coherence have not yet been achieved regarding this political function of the solidarity economy, and that the necessary linkage between different projects (Coraggio 2012)[30] is still to be attained.

Last, in relation to the organizational field, the solidarity economy supports criticism of the "legal straitjacketing" that surrounds the social economy concept and, on this point, comes closer to the interpretation of social enterprise applied by the EMES school (Defourny and Nyssens 2012). This conception of social enterprise employs three dimensions (economic, social, and participative) and its practice regards all firms that behave in accordance with these principles as falling within social enterprise.

---

30 Foe a deeper understanding of the political function of the social economy, see Coraggio (2012); Pérez de Mendiguren and Etxezarreta (2016).

The Social Economy: A Valid Instrument for Social Transformation

As noted in the previous sections, the social economy has undergone a building process over the last forty years. But the limits of the social economy have also been exposed. We have presented modernizing contributions to broaden the social economy concept and delve deeper into its political function. The reflections we offer in the preceding paragraphs indicate that the social economy can have the capacity to become a valid instrument for social transformation.

Moreover, in the current situation of crisis, the social economy could play an important role. We are unquestionably facing a crisis of conjuncture. We are experiencing the age of globalization, and it is driven by neoliberalism. Global capitalism has total hegemony in this context. Enormous structural changes are being produced in the model of development, setting off multiple crises, above all in the world of work, the state, the field of finance, the global economy, the environment, and in the field of care. In our times inequalities and social exclusion are on the rise, the trend toward individualism is likewise gathering pace, and states are becoming ungovernable. But at the same time several initiatives are arising to confront these negative dynamics, forging solidarity, balancing the correlation of forces, and redistributing wealth. Within this context, the social economy must confront endeavors of the first order to find a way through economic and social inequalities while building another model of alternative development (Bouchard 2006). The social economy has demonstrated that it has the strengths to find a place for social values within daily practice (Lévesque 2004) and, indeed, the capacity to maintain a political perspective (Eme and Laville 1994).

The rise in influence that the social economy has achieved in recent years reveals that the space it currently occupies between the market and the state is far more than residual. Nonetheless, rather than concerning ourselves with the dimensions of the social economy, we should look to the potentiality this sector possesses to impact the institutional field. We certainly cannot consider the social economy strictly as a mere producer of goods and services, because it can also become an active agent in providing impetus for social and political coordination (Laville and Evers 2004). We could, additionally, make the social economy evolve into a useful instrument for social transformation.

But to do so, the social economy will have to unleash all its potentiality without occupying just a token position. We are aware that, in the present socioeconomic context, the social economy has two souls. Because it is integrated into the capitalist system, in certain respects the differences between capitalist firms and the social economy are becoming fewer. But the latter does continue to maintain different features that lie outside the logic of capitalism, which can constitute important levers for thinking and showing that alternatives for the future are possible.

Then again, the situation of the social economy is ambivalent: on the one hand, it has been assimilated and tends toward a lack of differentiation, while on the other, it is or can be an incubator of alternatives. That means that the future of the social economy will depend on the steps taken in one direction or the other. The main objective, therefore, must be to maintain the basic principles, enhance and update them, and place them, meanwhile, at the service of social transformation. That requires rooting out certain vices and inertias from the social economy while improving those aspects that are well on track.

The starting point for achieving that target is recognition of the social economy as a valuable experience. It has traveled on a path of democratic practice in firms with all the accompanying contributions, fluctuations, and contradictions, and is still holding the road. What is more, it has met its commitments with economic, social, and cultural development at the local level. From that perspective, in terms of capitalist standardization, it stands out as a singular socioeconomic experience of its own making that offers interesting pointers at the present historical moment.

In our view, therefore, the social economy has a strategic nature within socioeconomic organization and constitutes a valid tool for keeping a distance from the economistic perspective and working to incorporate a different, more human model and other more social values within economic development as a whole. To realize that aim, once the basic pillars of the social economy have been restored so that it may become a strategic element of social transformation, we would then have to adapt that supporting structure to the new times.

The social economy must work in two different directions. The first involves extending the unique socioeconomic experience, striving to achieve an increasingly radical business democracy, and no longer placing the emphasis on growth, but rather on qualitative aspects. The second, however, implies strengthening and renewing social commitments. These directions are complementary and around them we want to galvanize different areas of work: namely, developing participatory democracy, cultivating ideas, and stimulating debate and social and cooperative training; this, in turn, means guaranteeing decent working conditions, respecting the environment, incorporating the social and cultural characteristics of the milieu, and taking part in cooperation for world development and in the construction of local development.

Conclusion

The social economy has been strengthened in a process that stretches over forty years and this is largely due to the identification of the sector with particular legal entities. The fact that it was defined in this manner has raised its prominence, facilitating measurement via statistical data and a clearer delimitation of public policy targets to promote the sector.

Indeed, in some countries the social economy concept can be said to have achieved institutional representation and important public and juridical recognition. It has been consolidated significantly in the Basque Country, Spain, France, and Europe. Implementing the concept in these territories owes its success to the deployment of institutional representatives, the development of institutional resolutions, research, and progress on the legal front. However, as is confirmed in the two research works that we have used as a reference, changing concepts are employed to mention entities of this kind, depending on the country in question. It is immediately clear that the social economy commands different levels of recognition in various countries in Europe and that surrounding this concept other similar concepts are engaged in some sort of competition.

Yet it can be said that in Europe a closer relationship has been forged among the different concepts that are in dispute around the social economy. They still maintain some distinguishing characteristics: the third sector concept excludes agents that work in the market and welcomes volunteers; and the term social economy, while it does not exclude the market, is distinguished by its collective democratic activity at the service of people.

We must also underline the fact that the limits of the social economy concept are palpable, and the solidarity economy offers innovative proposals to go beyond those boundaries and seek renewal, above all when it comes to enhancing the social economy concept, extending its political function, and helping to construct a new theoretical corpus that can take on the current hegemonic economic theory. Essentially, as soon as the solidarity economy becomes a social practice, this concept requires a resocialization and repoliticization of the economy.

From all the preceding reflections, our conclusion would be that in this era of globalization dominated by capitalist hegemony, the social economy can become a valid instrument for social transformation. What is more, in the present situation of crisis, the social economy has the capacity to play a leading role in the construction of a different more human model of development. But for that to take place the social economy must go beyond lip service and unleash all its potentiality for social transformation. The challenge is not only to maintain the basic principles, but to enhance and update them, placing social economy policy at the service of social transformation. In our view, the social economy should work in two different directions. The first involves extending the unique socioeconomic experience, striving to achieve an increasingly radical business democracy, and no longer placing the emphasis on growth, but on qualitative aspects. The second, however, requires the strengthening and renewal of social commitments.

Bibliography

Barea, José, and José Luis Monzón. 1995. Las Cuentas Satélite de la Economía Social en España: una primera aproximación. Valencia: CIRIEC-España.

———. 2007. Manual para la elaboración de las cuentas satélite de las empresas de la Economía Social: Cooperativas y Mutuas. Valencia: CIRIEC-España.

Bouchard, Marie J. 2006. "De l'experimentation à l'institutionnalisation positive, l'innovation sociale dans le logement communautaire au Québec." Annales de l'économie publique, sociale et cooperative 77, no. 2: 139–66.

Brunsson, Nils. 1989. *The Organisation of Hypocrisy: Talk, Decisions and Actions in Organisations.* Chichester: John Wiley.

Coraggio, José Luis, ed. 2009 *¿Qué es lo económico? Materiales para un debate necesario contra el fatalismo.* Buenos Aires: Ciccus.

———. 2011. *Economía social y solidaria. El trabajo antes que el capital.* Quito: Abya Yala.

———. 2012. "Las tres corrientes vigentes de pensamiento y acción dentro del campo de la Economía Social y Solidaria (ESS): Sus diferentes alcances." At *http://www.socioeco. org/bdf/es/corpus_document/fiche-document-2124.html* (last accessed November 26, 2017).

Chaves, Rafael. 1997. "Economía política de la economía social. Una visión de la literatura económica reciente." CIRIEC-España: Revista de Economía Pública, Social y Cooperativa 25: 141–62.

————. 1999. "La economía social como enfoque metodológico, como objeto de estudio
y como disciplina científica." CIRIEC-España: Revista de Economía Pública, Social y Cooperativa 33: 115–39.

Dacheux, Eric, and Daniel Goujon. 2011. *Principes d´ économie solidaire.* Paris: Ellipses.

Defourny, Jacques, and Marthe Nyssens. 2012. "El enfoque EMES de la empresa social desde una perspective comparada." *CIRIEC-España: Revista de Economía Pública, Social y Cooperativa* 75: 7–34.

Eme, Bernard, and Jean-Louis Laville, eds. 1994. Cohésion Sociale et emploi. Paris: Desclée de Brower.

Etxezarreta, Enekoitz, and Jon Morandeira. 2012. "Consideraciones conceptuales sobre la Economía Social a la luz de la Ley 5/2011." *Revista vasca de economía social/ Gizarte ekonomiaren euskal aldizkaria* 8: 7–36.

Etxezarreta, Enekoitz, Juan Carlos Pérez de Mendiguren, and Jon Morandeira. 2014. "Sobre el concepto de Economía Social y su proceso de consolidación." In Economía Social Vasca y Crisis Económica: Análisis de su evolución socioeconómica entre 2009 y 2013, edited by Ignacio Bretos and José María Pérez de Uralde. Donostia-San Sebastián: OVES.

Fajardo, Gemma. 2012. "El fomento de la economía social en la legislación española." *REVESCO: Revista de Estudios Cooperativos* 107: 58–97.

Itçaina, Xabier. 2017. "Ipar Euskal Herriko Gizarte Ekonomiaz." At http://www.oves-geeb.com/eu/noticias-eu/detalle-eu/ipar-euskal-herriko-gizarte-ekonomiaz-1011 (last accessed November 25, 2017).

Laville, Jean-Louis. 2013. "Économie sociale et solidaire, capitalisme et changement démocratique." In *Vers une théorie de l'économie sociale et solidaire,* edited by David Hiez and Eric Lavillunière. Collection: Droit & économie sociale et solidaire. Paris: Editions Larcier.

————. 2004. "El marco conceptual de la Economía social y solidaria." In *Economía social y solidaria: Una visión europea*, edited by
Jean-Louis Laville. Buenos Aires. Fundación OSDE; Universidad Nacional de General Sarmiento-Altamira.

Laville, Jean-Louis, and Adalbert Evers, eds. 2004. The Third Sector
in Europe. Cheltenham, UK and Northampton, MA: Edward
Elgar.

Lévesque, Benoît. 2004. "Les entreprises d´économie sociale, plus
porteuses d´innovations sociales que les autres?" In Le devel-
oppement social au rythme de l´innovation. Québec: Presses
de l´Université du Québec et Fonds de recherche sur la société
et la culture.

Meyer, John, and Brian Rowan. 1977. "Institutional Organizations:
Formal Structure as Myth and Ceremony." *American Journal of
Sociology* 83: 340–63.

Monzón, José Luis. 2003. "El cooperativismo en la historia de la
literatura económica." CIRIEC-España: Revista de Economía
Pública, Social y Cooperativa 44: 9–32.

————. 2006. "Economía Social y conceptos afines: fronteras borrosas y ambigüedades conceptuales del Tercer Sector." CIRIEC-
España: Revista de Economía Pública, Social y Cooperativa
56: 9–24.

————, ed. 2010. Las grandes cifras de la Economía Social en España. Ámbito, entidades y cifras clave año 2008. Valencia:
CIRIEC.

————. 2016. "La economía social en la literatura económica y en los
hechos. 30 años del CIRIEC-España." CIRIEC-España: Revista de Economía Pública, Social y Cooperativa 88: 287–307.

Monzón, José Luis, and Rafael Chaves. 2012. The Social Economy
in the European Union. Brussels: European Economic and
Social Committee.

————. 2017. Recent Evolutions of the Social Economy in the European Union. Brussels: European Economic and Social Committee.

Pérez de Mendiguren, Juan Carlos, and Enekoitz Etxezarreta. 2015. "Sobre el concepto de economía social y solidaria: aproximaciones desde Europa y América Latina." *Revista de Economía Mundial* 40: 123–44.

————. 2016. "Otros modelos de empresa en la economía solidaria: entre la retórica y la práctica." *Lan Harremanak Aldizkaria* 33: 227–52.

Pérez de Mendiguren, Juan Carlos, Enekoitz Etxezarreta, and Luis Guridi. 2009. "Economía Social, Empresa Social y Economía Solidaria: diferentes conceptos para un mismo debate." *Papeles de Economía Solidaria* 1: 1–41.

Pérez De Uralde, José María. 2014. "La inaplicación de la Ley de Economía Social en un contexto de crisis económica: Algunas interpretaciones y propuestas." CIRIEC-España: Revista de Economía Pública, Social y Cooperativa 81: 33–59.

Polanyi, Karl. 2007. *The Great Transformation*. New York and Toronto: Farrar & Rinehart.

Salamon, Lester M., and S. Wojciech Sokolowsky. 2014. The Third Sector in Europe: Towards a Consensus Conceptualization. TSI Working Paper Series no. 2/2014, European Union. Brussels: Third Sector Impact.

2

A New Framework for the Third Sector in Euskadi in the Context of the European Union

M. IGONE ALTZELAI

It is common knowledge that Basque society has traditionally possessed a broad social fabric composed of an abundance of organizations that emerged from civic initiatives to provide responses to specific situations, problems, or needs, and that continues to be the case. We call this the *third sector* or, more accurately, the *third social sector*. That is the wording used in the explanatory memorandum to Law 6/2016, May 12, on the Third Social Sector in Euskadi, which defines what it terms as "third social sector organizations in Euskadi and social initiative organizations."

This is a law rooted in the exclusive jurisdiction that the Autonomous Community of the Basque Country (Euskadi) enjoys with regard to: social assistance; educational, cultural, artistic, charitable, welfare, and similar foundations and associations, as long as they carry out their duties mainly in the Basque Country; cooperatives and friendly societies not integrated into the welfare system; and community development, the status of women, policy covering children, young people, and senior citizens. According to the framework of the legal structure for distributing competences between the Spanish state and the Autonomous Community of Euskadi, its Statute of Autonomy (also known as the Statute of Gernika) confers exclusive jurisdiction on it in these areas. Indeed, Law 12/2008, December 5, on Social Services had previously introduced what is known as the "third social action sector within our legal system," which was defined later by Decree 283/2012, of December 11, whereby the Forum for Civil Dialogue was constituted and regulated.

At the state level, the approach is different. The Spanish legal system has one law on the social economy and another on the third sector. Law 5/2011 of March 29 on the Social Economy sets up a legal framework for "social economy entities" and provides mechanisms of dialogue for these organizations with the public administrations. Law 43/2015 of October 9 on the Third Social Action Sector, meanwhile, establishes a regulatory framework for "third social action sector entities." Disadvantaged social groups placed in a situation of vulnerability or at risk of exclusion constitute the central object of their attention. The purpose of this law is also to regulate dialogue between these entities and the general state administration.

Within the European Union (EU), there is also regulation on the social economy. The legal framework here is different and drafted from the perspective of a single market that needs growth that is inclusive, more ethical, and more social. The basic reference is embodied in the Communication from the Commission to the European Parliament, the Council, the European Economic and Social Committee, and the Committee of the Regions, under the title *Social Business Initiative: creating a favorable climate for social enterprises, key stakeholders in the social economy, and innovation* (henceforth, *Initiative*) (European Commission 2011b).

In the European Union a communication is not binding, it is not a standard. It does however constitute an important legal instrument that serves to determine the position of the European Commission regarding the measures that the other institutions in the EU should adopt. In this case, the *Initiative* demonstrates a will to support a "highly competitive social market economy," for which purpose the European Commission takes the social economy and social innovation as central elements, both where territorial cohesion is concerned, as well as the search for solutions to social problems. Prominent among these aims is, specifically, the fight against poverty and exclusion that the European Commission specifies in its document *Strategy Europe 2020* (2010a), in *Europe 2020 flagship initiative Innovation Union*, Brussels (2010b), in *The European Platform against Poverty and Social Exclusion* (2010c), and in *Single Market Act* (2011a). In this context, in line with the purposes stated, the *Initiative* defines the notion of a social enterprise as an agent of the social economy. This concept of social enterprise is embodied in (EU) Regulation No 346/2013 of the European Parliament and the Council, of April 17, 2013, concerning the European social entrepreneurship funds, the intention being to regulate funds that invest in enterprises promoting social changes, and offering innovative solutions to social problems.

Given this wide variety of rules, bodies, and institutions, one wonders whether the various bodies referred to, the third social sector organizations, social initiative organizations, third social action sector entities, social economy entities, and social enterprises, are equivalent legal categories or not, and about the relation that exists among them. But this question, in turn, leads one to another preliminary issue, which requires analysis of the interrelation between the social economy and the third sector.

Against this backdrop, the objective of the present chapter is to provide an answer to these matters, although I do not intend to conduct a detailed analysis of each of the legal constructs mentioned. Faced with this plurality of social economy and third sector organizations, the aim is rather to develop a valid approach for them all that contains efficient criteria for interpretation and serves to verify whether a specific entity belongs to the area of the social economy or of the third sector. In other words, my study seeks to offer an instrument by which to observe the common features that define the agents in all this special differentiated sector of the economy.

Third Sector and Social Economy

Several studies analyze the relation between the third sector and the social economy, and debate as to how to possibly identify them, given that they share broadly common spaces. That is why I question whether they are two different spheres or two components of one and the same reality.

The third sector (also known as the third social sector) and the social economy are linked by common characteristics and objectives. In both cases private organizations participate that focus their activity on improving society and attending to the needs of people rather than the needs of capital. These organizations tend to apply management criteria addressed at optimizing their activity and not toward attaining a higher economic margin. They seek benefit for the community and not for themselves. Their intervention is set on increasing profitability and resource utilization and not on controlling the market, and they prioritize social, not economic results; when there *are* positive outcomes, they reinvest them in the organization itself (Crespo 2013, 66).

However, a distinction is still made between the social economy and the third sector, despite the lack of homogeneity in their composition, their classification, and their nomenclature, and the lack of clear criteria in their cataloging.

On the one hand, the social economy has been regarded historically as having its origins in cooperatives devoted to consumption and production at the end of both the eighteenth and nineteenth centuries that championed a different conception of the economy, departing from the idea of pure private interest as the driving force of the economy. For some, even today, the cooperative movement constitutes the backbone of the social economy (Monzón 2006). But it is also true that in the 1970s a broader conception of social economy began to develop that, taking cooperatives as its point of departure, spread to all forms of organization that, in their operations, question the logic of capitalist development (Argudo 2002, 247).

On the other hand, the third sector has traditionally been considered to have originated in private and sometimes religious initiatives, and then to have gradually incorporated new altruistic features in defense of social justice, leading it to become more prominent socially and assume responsibility, alongside the public administrations, for the community's welfare. This sector has evolved, improving its organization, introducing new management methods, and achieving greater sustainability in its projects, without abandoning the purposes that led to its creation. Thus, this sector—which has been characterized for some time as being scarcely professionalized, relying on a strong presence of volunteers, suffering from atomization, and possessing weak structures—has managed to improve its coordination and to organize itself to become a force with economic potential.

All these movements developed thanks to the activity of organizations and private initiative that has found very different ways of expression, providing the population with welfare, and acting on defining principles such as solidarity, a nonprofit status, and the fight against inequality. Their track record in recent years shows us a clear collaboration between the private and the public spheres in which the choice, to a large extent, has been to outsource many of their services and entrust their management to entities of this nature. This has meant that the latter have largely been characterized by their commitment to the production of goods and services of public interest, thereby occupying an important place within the economy of a country.

This practice has meant that today all these organizations of a social character must deal with commercial companies that, driven to secure maximum benefits in their own interest, engage in competition with them. Against this background, this new social sector is targeting productive, nonprofit, business organizations that combine the public and the private; attempting to overcome a situation of single dependency on the administration, they develop private investment arising from greater co-responsibility from civil society and plan new ways of funding themselves and managing the activity they carry out.

These changes in economic management do not prevent them from defending their usual principles. But this process has managed to generate greater economic value from the activity these organizations engage in and that has led to an increasing identification between the social economy and the third sector (Defourny and Nyssens 2010, 39). They have grown and developed side by side and, in a sense, they can both now be said to form part of the same concept. This is the exact European focus that has just been incorporated into the social economy, referred to in the English-speaking world as *nonprofit organizations*, which were traditionally identified in some countries with the third sector. Under this new conception, the social economy is composed of organizations that operate on the principle that there is no profit distribution (Chaves and Monzón, 2001), while other entities that do not apply this principle form part of the public sector, or the capitalist sector.

The European Union Model

As noted, in the European Union there is a unitary rather than dual approach, which is connected to the social economy, and the figure of reference for determining its scope is the *social enterprise*. This figure has developed over time and is defined in the *Initiative* (European Commission 2011b) through the stipulation of three requirements: A social objective of common interest that constitutes the raison d'être of the economic activity social enterprises develop; reinvestment of the profits of these organizations or companies, principally in carrying out their social objective (or a nonprofit motive); and a mode of organization or of ownership based on democratic or participatory principles, or with a social justice orientation.

The European model of social enterprise is built on these three foundations. That is how making any reference to the typology or legal form of social companies has been circumvented. This is perfectly logical, given the panorama of widely heterogeneous types of entities, bodies, and companies that exist in the different member states of the EU in the social economy area. The European Commission has opted not to impinge on the formal aspects, as that would prove tremendously complicated and problematic. It has preferred instead to develop avenues that assist in grasping the reality of this highly diverse typology. To this end it has focused its attention on the traits it deems to be common to all the types of organizations or entities that might be regarded as having a social mission.

It should be noted that the conception in this model does not represent a new standard, because such a model has in fact already been tested. The British government, with the *Social Enterprise: A Strategy for Success* it initiated in 2002, set up a model based on two fundamental features: the objectives should be social, and most of the profits must be reinvested in the company or in society.

The basic outline of the European Commission's social enterprise notion has already taken concrete shape in the rule expressed in (EU) Regulation 346/2013 on the European social entrepreneurship funds. In Europe there is an increasing number of investors interested in such companies, and not only in the pursuit of financial profitability, because a social investment market has been emerging that is comprised partly of investment funds that provide funding to social enterprises pursuing solutions to social problems. The regulation is aimed at these funds, and must, naturally, furnish a clear definition of what these firms are, with the necessary guarantees of legal security (article 3.1.d). They are subject to the following requirements: the prime aim of the company consists of having a positive social effect, rather than generating profits for its owners or their members; its operations must provide goods and services to the market and its profits should fundamentally be utilized to achieve social objectives; and the company should be managed responsibly and transparently, involving, above all, the participation of its employees, consumers, and parties interested in its commercial activities.

It is important to underscore the fact that the notion of social enterprise has received a legal categorization and been included in a legal rule that has a general reach, (EU) Regulation No 346/2013, and that this is binding in its entirety and directly applicable in all member states. The social enterprise concept has thereby been integrated into EU law for all the states in the European Union (Altzelai 2016, 21). That does not necessarily mean that the systems and defining criteria of the organizations or social enterprises in all the states must match completely. But it does imply that they must at least be compatible with the European model. This stands as a reference point for all of them.

This configuration scheme for the social enterprise displays interesting advantages in its application. Its flexible nature constitutes its most positive noteworthy feature, as it makes it possible to welcome in a diversity of entities, organizations, and companies, regardless of their legal form. Thus, any body of any type can potentially receive the social enterprise rating providing that it meets these few basic requirements and they are appropriately validated.

As regards the European Union, when it comes to the manner of verifying compliance with the fundamental features, some mechanisms that can act as a guide for the remaining legal orders have already been put in place. Accordingly, (EU) Regulation 346/2013 (article 3.1.d) requires that the social objective of common interest, preference for reinvestment in the execution of that aim, and the organization or system of ownership of the firm, based on democratic or participatory principles or with a social justice orientation, are expressly enshrined in some of the company's founding documents, in the public deed, in its statutes, or in any other document. The European Commission, meanwhile, is still pondering the finalization and implementation of a common European statute for social enterprises, its concern being that it should prove simple, attractive, and capable of responding to the needs of social entrepreneurs.

The Spanish Legislation Approach: A Dual Model?

Unlike the European approach, the Spanish legal system follows a dual model that distinguishes between the social economy and the third sector. Law 5/2011 on the Social Economy and Law 43/2015 on the Third Social Action Sector regulate social economy entities, and bodies in the third social action sector, respectively, which are referred to below. Faced with this duality, though, there are those (Altzelai 2016) who propose adopting a fresh reading of these laws, in such a way that their interpretation be in keeping with the European approach.

Social Economy Entities

Law 5/2011 on the Social Economy is aimed at social economy entities. Its objective is to establish a common legal framework for these bodies and to determine suitable measures to promote them. This law, however, contains no express definition of social economy entities, and this creates problems when it comes to identifying its scope of application. This obliges us to deduce from its articles the meaning that must be conferred on this legal figure.

Article 2 of the law provides a brief definition of the social economy as "all economic and business activities that entities conduct within the private sphere and, in agreement with the principles reflected in article 4, that pursue either the collective interest of their members, or the general or social economic interest, or both." These are the guiding principles: the primacy of people and of the social purpose over capital, the prioritization of decision-making that depends upon people and their contributions of work and services rather than on their contributions to social capital; the application of results obtained from economic activity mainly in accordance with the work or service performed and, where appropriate, with the social purpose the entity aims to meet; the promotion of solidarity internally and within society; and independence vis-à-vis the public administrations. Article 5 then provides a list of legal entities that it regards as belonging to the social economy: cooperative companies; friendly societies; foundations; associations that conduct economic activity; labor companies; insertion companies; special employment centers; and fishermen's guilds; and agricultural processing companies.

This list is not meant to be definitive. Article 5 goes on to add that *singular entities* created by specific rules that are governed by the principles of article 4 could also form part of the social economy.

Indeed, in Spain, the Spanish Red Cross (Royal Decree 415/1996) and the Spanish National Organization for the Blind (Organización Nacional de Ciegos Españoles), ONCE (Royal Decree 358/1991) have been granted this status. Caritas Spain is the Official Confederation of bodies devoted to charitable and social action attached to the Catholic Church in Spain, but it was not created by any specific Spanish provision.

The second section of article 5 likewise makes it possible for organizations that conduct economic business activity, and whose rules of operation match those guiding principles and are included in the catalogue of entities that the Ministry of Work and Immigration must prepare, to be regarded as social economy entities. The law states that this catalogue must be kept updated and coordinated with catalogues that may exist at the autonomous community level. But this possibility has not been developed.

A matter for concern is that the social economy law does not expressly say that the entities included in the list in article 5 should substantiate observance of the guiding principles of article 4. Thus, at first glance, it may appear that the Spanish legislators presume that the entities on the list are already operating in line with these principles, endorsed simply because they have adopted a specific legal form (Arrieta 2014, 34). The requirement to obey these principles is expressly addressed toward any other organizations that, maintaining another legal form, aspire to obtain the attribute of belonging to the social economy.

Both the content and the systematics employed by the law on the social economy have triggered several critical reactions. One such criticism refers to the list of social economy entities considered in article 5 (Paniagua 2011, 165; Paz 2012, 93; Sánchez and Pérez, 2015, 37). Another concerns the guiding principles of the social economy defined in article 4 (Fajardo 2012b, 280; Paniagua 2011, 155). In my view this makes it necessary to clarify our understanding of these principles in the law on the social economy and of ways of determining the notion of social economy entities envisaged in the law, adjusting them to an interpretation consistent with the European model (Altzelai 2016, 24).

Entities in the Third Social Action Sector

The law governing the third social action sector establishes legislation, at state level, for all the entities within this area. Its main aim is to strengthen and correct the capacity of the third sector in which policies against poverty and exclusion are concerned. It seeks "to eradicate the existing inequalities that continue to affect the most vulnerable groups in society." In consequence, the law regulates the entities, their fundamental principles, and their participation in the devising of social policies.

In article 2 the law defines third social action sector entities as "organizations of a private nature created through social or civic initiative or, under different modalities, that follow criteria of solidarity and of social participation, for aims of general interest with a nonprofit motive, supporting the recognition and exercise of civil rights, and of the economic, social, or cultural rights of people and groups that suffer conditions of vulnerability or are at risk of social exclusion." In this case, in contrast to what occurs with social economy entities, the definition fits the European Union model.

The most popular third social action sector entities in the Spanish state are Cáritas, the Red Cross, and ONCE, the Spanish National Organization for the Blind (García Montoro 2015, 2). But there are also others, and they normally group together creating joint action platforms. Such is the Third Sector Platform, comprising seven organizations: The Platform of Non-Governmental Social Action Organizations (Plataforma de ONG de Acción Social, POAS); the Volunteer Platform of Spain (Plataforma de Voluntariado de España, PVE), the European Anti-Poverty Network, Spain (EAPN-ES); the Spanish Committee of Representatives of Persons with Disabilities (Comité Español de Representantes de Personas con Discapacidad, CERMI); Spanish Cáritas, the Spanish Red Cross, and the Spanish National Organization for the Blind (ONCE). This platform was accredited in 2013 as a civil society interlocutor that would communicate its needs to the Spanish government through the Commission for Civil Dialogue.

Nonetheless, as mentioned above, the Spanish Red Cross, the Spanish National Organization for the Blind, and Cáritas Spain are recognized as singular entities in the framework of the law on the social economy. As a result, precisely the most important entities in this area receive dual recognition as social economy entities and third social action sector entities. This leads us to conclude that, fundamentally, this distinction between social economy and third sector does not appear necessary, which renders a dual model based on that distinction rather pointless.

According to the stipulations of article 4 of the Law on the Third Social Action Sector, "regardless of their legal nature" the following defining qualities constitute the governing principles of third social action sector entities:

a) Having their own legal personality.

b) Being of a private judicial nature.

c) Not having a profit motive and being of an altruistic nature.

d) Guaranteeing democratic participation.

e) Acting in a transparent manner.

f) Developing their activities with full guarantees of autonomy in their management and decision-making vis-à-vis the general state administration.

g) Contributing to making social cohesion effective by means of civic participation in social action grounded in volunteerism.

h) Acting on principles of equality of opportunity and treatment, and nondiscrimination, with special attention to the principle of equality between men and women.

i) Following objectives and conducting activities of general interest, defined as such in a regulation having the force of law and, in all cases, including the following activities of social interest:

1. Providing attention to people with comprehensive social and/ or health attention needs.

2. Providing attention to people with educational or labor insertion needs.

3. Promotion of civil safety and the prevention of crime.

I do not assume with this list that the aim of this law is to assign tasks to third sector entities that know well enough what the needs of the citizens they service are; the aim is, rather, to promote the institutional participation of these entities in the general state administration (Calvo 2015, 3), to establish measures to develop these bodies and, in particular, to adopt an energizing program for third social action sector entities that the government ought to have endorsed during the twelve-month period prior to the passing of the law, and that it has still, however (as of 2018), not implemented.

One of the bodies for the institutional participation in the general state administration of third sector entities is the Commission for Civil Dialogue with the Third Sector Platform referred to above, which will, as foreseen in article 9 of this law, be legally regulated for the purposes of institutionalizing permanent collaboration, cooperation, and dialogue with the relevant ministry (it has not yet been regulated).

In sum, the approach of the Spanish legal system, based on a dual model that makes a distinction between the social economy and the third sector, has already been surpassed by current circumstances, and it does not match the European model (Strategy Europe 2020). The third sector is still considered to be financially dependent on the state and not as a complex and ambivalent sector (Marbán and Rodríguez 2013, 63) with broad functions that take in social protection, social investment, and social innovation.

Social Initiative Organizations in Euskadi

Law 6/2016 of May 12on the Third Social Sector in Euskadi aims primarily to establish the statute of the organizations it forms part of, moving forward in identifying organizations with a social initiative and intervention beyond the definition of their sector as nonprofit, recognizing the importance of their social contribution (particularly in the field of social policies), and their right to participate actively in them.

This legislation also has other objectives, including: the systematization and reinforcement of cooperation mechanisms with the public sector and the business sector; the consolidation of different spaces of dialogue with the public sector and with other social agents in which the social sector is or ought to be present; and the standardization and fortification of tools and policies for promoting the third social sector (or social sector) through the public administrations and other social agents.

Thus, this law involves a diversity of sectors. It draws in, obviously, the third or social sector, organizations of a social initiative and intervention, and the civic field (family associations, the old, the young, women, immigrants, social action, and international development cooperation, among others), but also extends to the public sector (Basque public administrations and legislative bodies in the Autonomous Community of the Basque Country) and the business sector, companies, and organizations.

For the purposes of this law (article 2), the following bodies form part of this third sector in Euskadi: organizations based on social initiative (defined in article 3); second or higher-level networks or organizations representing these organizations; and other types of organizations, providing that they carry out activities in the social intervention area and meet certain conditions (set out in article 2.3). They are all private, self-governed, and self-managed nonprofit organizations with a legal structure and personality, and have been recorded in the corresponding register; they are devoted to voluntary action and their headquarters and activity are in the

Basque Country. Their main purpose is to promote social inclusion and development cooperation. The law defines the features that characterize organizations based on social initiative as the following: (a) they are totally or partially based on voluntary action; (b) they form part of civil society, and have emerged from and for it; (c) they are of a private nature, constituting a self-managed institution separate from the administration; (d) they are of a nonprofit nature, not pursuing the distribution of economic profits and reinvesting them in the organization's mission; and (e) they are based on participation for the purposes of decision-making, in accordance with the standard applicable to their legal form.

The autonomous legislating authority deemed it necessary both to bolster the actual structuration of the social sector and foster collaboration between it and the public sector and other sectors and agents, envisaging participation from networks in the social sector in the Forum for Civil Dialogue in Euskadi and in its Economic and Social Council.

The first chapter of the new law characterizes and gives shape to what it terms the "third social sector in Euskadi," comprising social initiative organizations that perform activities in the field of social intervention, including participation in the provision of services within the sphere of public responsibility that, in this area, are understood to be social services of general interest. The creation of a census of these organizations in the Basque Country is envisaged and the supporting principles for this are set out.

Chapter 2 specifies the principle of civil dialogue, providing for the participation of this sector in the development, execution, monitoring, and evaluation of public policies in the field of social intervention. Such participation is expressed, among other means, through the Forum for Civil Dialogue in Euskadi and the Basque Economic and Social Council.

Chapter 3 makes advances in defining the reach of the relation between the social sector and the public sector, this being established in terms of cooperation and collaboration in the execution of social action policies. The law concretizes the need to cooperate both in the management of systems of public responsibility and spaces of interaction between systems, and in the provision of services of public responsibility.

To coordinate this relation of cooperation and collaboration, the regulation refers to three instruments stipulated in Law 12/2008 of December 5 on Social Services: special social concertation regimes, conventions, and framework collaboration agreements. It also establishes a series of additional obligations for organizations that collaborate with public administrations to ensure that they are ethically and transparently managed.

Lastly, chapter 4 considers action to promote the third social sector in the Basque Country taken by the public sector, including measures of support for the development of infrastructures, the making of investments, stimulation of the economic activity of third social sector organizations, and collaboration with the business sector.

The Basque Model within the European Union Model

The legal framework that shapes the law on the third social sector in Euskadi addresses entities in the social area that it calls *social initiative organizations*. The law, indeed, might more accurately have been called the "law on social initiative in Euskadi," instead of the allusion made to the third sector. This would perhaps have been more in keeping with its spirit and unitary approach, because the reference to the third sector can lead to confusion. It may create the impression that, in correspondence with the Spanish legal system, the Basque law follows a dual model based on the distinction between the social economy and the third sector. Whereas, as opposed to the Spanish legislation, my understanding is that the notion of *social initiative organization* in the Basque law fits in with the European Union's conception of *social enterprise*, contained in the *Initiative* (European Commission 2011b) and in (EU) Regulation No. 346/2013.

In this regard, a first shadow of doubt may understandably be raised as to whether "social initiative organization" and "social enterprise" mean the same thing. It is also natural to think, perhaps, that by the term "organization" the Basque legislating authority meant to refer to a broader concept that may include business and non-business organizations. These and other hypotheses that could have been formulated lead me to shed some light on this matter as a preparatory step to building a valid interpretative approach.

To this end, and taking as our starting point the fact that, in principle, norms should be interpreted from the meaning that their wording transmits (article 3.1 Civil Code), I will start by contending that, on one hand, the word "organization" communicates the idea of a collectivity considered as a unit. The term is normally used to refer to any corporation, company, institution, and so on. It is also often employed as a synonym of a legal person. On the other hand, the term "enterprise" is generally used to refer to organizations devoted to economic activities, as well as to refer to legal persons (Harding 2004, 40). As a result, to begin with, it is difficult to overlook the fact that both terms indicate very broad concepts that can, to a great degree, converge. Although the Basque legislators preferred to employ the word "organization" instead of "enterprise," we can and should consider both terms as fulfilling a similar function and therefore they may be used as equivalents (Arrieta 2014, 39). In Basque law we do in fact find some other signs, such as the allusions to companies in article 2, that lead us to draw this conclusion.

Within the European Union, the *Initiative* (European Commission 2011b) and (EU) Regulation No 346/2013 provide for a social enterprise model based on three structuring principles or components: a social objective of common interest: the reinvestment of profits, or a nonprofit motive; and governance. While the structuring features of articles 3 and 2 of the Law on the Third Social Sector in Euskadi do not exactly follow the same systematics, it is a matter of interest to find out whether the content of the law can indeed mesh with them. Let us see if a connection or equivalence can be established between the former and the latter.

As the first of the components that structure a social enterprise, the *Initiative* (European Commission 2011b) requires that there be a social objective of common interest. It states that such an aim must be the raison d'être of the (more or less commercial) action these enterprises are engaged in, which often results in a high degree of social innovation. Therefore, here we have a straightforward match, given the references made in article 2.1 and features (a) and (b) of article 3 of the Basque law, as mentioned in the previous section.

The second of the components that define a social enterprise in the EU framework demands that the profits should "principally" be reinvested in the realization of the social objective of common interest (article 3.1.d.iii of (EU) Regulation 346/2013). The requirement is not that they be totally reinvested in achieving that aim, because some allowance is made for a degree of sharing. This flexibility exists because otherwise entry to the various modalities of private funding would be impeded and there would be a risk that these companies' access to financing would be uniquely up to those who grant banking credit. Yet, despite this flexibility, the principle of preference for reinvestment is basic. It is, in fact, the key element that characterizes social enterprises and distinguishes them from other firms that are confined to developing strategies of corporate social responsibility (Katz and Page 2010, 89; Page and Katz 2011, 1381).

Where this second element is concerned, the Basque law is more forceful and more restrictive than the European regulation. It literally requires "the obligation to reinvest any eventual advantage in the organization's mission or, what amounts to the same thing, the impossibility of distributing profits" (article 3.d). Article 2.3.b) provides for the possibility of entities that do not meet some of the requirements stipulated in article 3 (in some cases) being considered members of the third social sector in Euskadi. Yet, even for those cases, the law expressly spells out the nonprofit nature of their activity as a condition. It states that "in the case of mercantile companies, statutory provision of the obligation to reinvest profits in activities that comprise their social objective will be understood to constitute a nonprofit approach." A systematic understanding that conforms to the EU model perhaps obliges us to propose a flexible reading of the law, implying, that is, the application of outcomes "principally" to the social purpose that the entity pursues, understanding likewise that the expression "social purpose" alludes to the *social objective* of common interest that the first structuring element mentions. This refocusing, in my view, could be feasible and should be called for.

The third defining element of the European notion of social enterprise demands a mode of organization or system of ownership based on principles that are democratic and participatory or geared to social justice, for example, with a low salary structure (European Commission 2011b, 3). Such an open formulation could open the way for all kinds of business structures and legal figures (Fajardo 2012b, 254). Sections (c) and (e) of article 2 of the Law on the Third Social Sector in Euskadi, therefore, referring to management autonomy and participation in management fall comfortably under this heading.

One can assert, then, taking as a foundation the aspects analyzed so far, that where the Basque law is concerned there is a legal framework that I believe is highly satisfactory, although I have also suggested some adjustments or proposals for improvement. As a model this legislation is not incompatible with its European counterpart, but it is a law that can however be interpreted as corresponding to a more restrictive framework, and one that should preferably be avoided.

Conclusion

Due to the reasons outlined, the view must be accepted that the new social economy represents a confluence of what has traditionally been regarded as the *third sector* and the *social economy*. Any regulation in this area today should therefore rest upon a unitary perspective on this sector of the economy. This approach makes it possible to encompass a whole host of organizations, entities, and companies that, as actors in this specific economic sector, share some of the same features.

In this respect, the European Union operates from a unitary approach at the core of which is the social enterprise defined simply and pragmatically for all member states and all kinds of entities.

The EU model defines the social enterprise in accordance with three constituent elements: a social objective of common interest; a preference for reinvesting profits toward this aim (a nonprofit motive); and governance. This simplicity provides the advantage of flexibility, as it enables the integration of highly diverse organizations rooted in all manner of legal forms.-

The Spanish legal system, however, basically follows a dual approach that distinguishes between the social economy and the third sector. This produces problems, so I propose making adjustments to this that I consider unavoidable, to fit in with the EU framework. In my understanding, with a flexible reading of the regulation it would be possible to develop a systematic interpretation to confer unity on the system, in line with the European legal framework. Above all, it is necessary to steer clear of the intra-regulatory inconsistencies that arise from a literal interpretation of the Spanish law.

The Autonomous Community of the Basque Country, in contrast, has developed a unitary approach that takes the new social economy into account. This approach can be comfortably incorporated in the European Union model, although the latter proves to be more restrictive than the Basque model.

Despite the variety of regulations, institutions, and organizations that I have referred to throughout this work (third social sector organizations, third social action sector entities, social economy entities, and social enterprises), I understand that they are equivalent legal categories, actors in the new social economy that must fit in with the outline and basic principles of the social enterprise model designed in the European Commission's *Initiative, Creating a favorable climate for social enterprises.*

As a final comment I would add that nothing stands in the way of any region, through the national law in each state, possessing its own model that may differ from the EU model, so long as they are both compatible. In addition to the legal perspective, on pragmatic grounds, one should not underestimate the impact that the EU notion of social enterprise has for our organizations. It is advisable for our organizations to exhibit a similar profile or for ours, at least, to fit in with theirs. A matching or comparable model in our national law might provide them with an interesting advantage. One should not forget that in 2013 the Council of the European Union endorsed the rules that will govern cohesion policy investments in the European Union for the period 2014–2020, with important investment in the social economy and social enterprises (European Commission 2013). This is yet another reason to understand that the EU model of social enterprise must be the basic reference that guides the legal configuration of what the law on the Third Social Sector in Euskadi designates as social initiative organizations or third social sector organizations.

Bibliography

Alfonso, Rosalía. 2010. "Algunas consideraciones en torno a la propuesta de ley marco de economía social." *REVESCO: Revista de Estudios Cooperativos* 102: 79–108.

———. 2015. "Los principios cooperativos como principios configuradores de la forma social cooperative." *CIRIEC-España: Revista Jurídica* 27: 1–36.

Altzelai, M. Igone. 2016. "Otro enfoque para las entidades de la economía social." *CIRIEC-España: Revista Jurídica* 28: 1–37.

Argudo, José Luis. 2002. "El tercer sector y la economía social." *Revista de Acciones e Investigaciones Sociales* 15: 239–63.

Arrieta, Francisco Javier. 2014. "Concreción de las entidades de la economía social." *REVESCO: Revista de Estudios Cooperativos* 116: 33–56.

Calvo, Juan. 2015. "La nueva Ley 43/2015 de 9 de octubre, del tercer sector de acción social: un nuevo marco de actuación para las entidades del tercer sector." *Aranzadi Doctrinal* 11: 1–9.

Chaves, Rafael, and José Luis Monzón. 2001. "Economía social y sector no lucrativo: actualidad científica y perspectivas." *CIRIEC-España* 37: 7–33.

Consejo de la Unión Europea. 2013. Reglamento (UE, EURATOM) N° 1311/2013 del Consejo, de 2 de diciembre de 2013, por el que se establece el marco financiero plurianual para el período 2014-2020, *DOUE* l 347, de 20.12.13.

Crespo, Teresa. 2013. "Una nueva relación del tercer sector y la economía social." *Cuadernos de Trabajo Social* 26, no. 1: 65–74.

Defourny, Jacques, and Marthe Nyssens. 2010. "Conceptions of Social Enterprise and Social Entrepreneurship in Europe and the United States: Convergences and Divergences." *Journal of Social Entrepreneurship* 1: 32–53.

European Commission, 2010a. *Communication from the Commission: Europe 2020. A Strategy for Smart, Sustainable and Inclusive Growth.* Brussels, 3.3.2010, COM(2010) 2020 final.

———. 2010b. *Communication from the Commission to the European Parliament, the Council, the European Economic and Social Committee and the Committee of the Regions Europe: 2020 flagship initiative Innovation Union.* Brussels 6.10.2010, COM(2010) 546 final.

———. 2010c. *Communication from the Commission to the European Parliament, the Council, the European Economic and social Committee and the Committee of the Regions: The European Platform against Poverty and Social Exclusion: A European framework for social and territorial cohesion.* Brussels 16.12.2010, COM(2010) 758 final.

———. 2011a. *Communication from the Commission to the European Parliament, the Council, the European Economic and social Committee and the Committee of the Regions: Single Market Act, Twelve levers to boost growth and strengthen confidence, Working together to create new growth.* Brussels 13.4.2011, COM(2011) 206 final.

———. 2011b. *Communication from the Commission to the European Parliament, the Council, the European Economic and Social Committee and the Committee of the Regions: Social Business Initiative Creating a favourable climate for social enterprises, key stakeholders in the social economy and innovation.* Brussels, 25.10.2011, COM(2011) 682 final.

————. 2013. *Communication from the Commission to the European Parliament, the Council, the European Economic and Social Committee and the Committee of the Regions: Towards Social Investment for Growth and Cohesion-including implementing the European Social Fund 2014– 2020.* Brussels, 20.2.2013, COM(2013) 83 final.

European Parliament. 2013. "Regulation (EU) No 346/2013 of the European Parliament and of the Council of 17 April 2013 on European social entrepreneurship funds." *OJEU* L 115, April 25: 18–38.

Fajardo, Gema. 2012a. "El concepto legal de economía social y la empresa social." *Revista Vasca de Economía Social: GEZKI* 8: 63–84.

————. 2012b. "Las empresas de economía social en la Ley 5/2011, de 29 de marzo." *Revista de Derecho de Sociedades* 38: 245–80.

García Montoro, Lourdes. 2015. "Nueva ley en apoyo de los sectores sociales marginados a través de las entidades del tercer sector de acción social." *Centro de Estudios de Consumo-Universidad de Casstilla la Mancha.* At www.uclm.es/centro/cesco (last accessed November 27, 2017).

Harding, Rebeca. 2004. "Social Enterprise: The New Economic Engine." *Business Strategy Review* 15, no. 4 (December): 39–43.

Katz, Robert A., and Antony Page. 2010. "The Role of Social Enterprise." *Vermont Law Review* 35: 59–104.

Marbán, Vicente, and Gregorio Rodríguez. 2013. "Sistemas mixtos de protección social. El tercer sector en la producción del bienestar." *Presupuesto y Gasto Público* 71: 61–82.

Monzón, José Luis. 2006. "Economía social y conceptos afines: fronteras borrosas y ambigüedades conceptuales del tercer sector." *CIRIEC-España: Revista de Economía Pública, Social y Cooperativa* 56: 9–24.

Page, Antony, and Robert A. Katz. 2012. "Is Social Enterprise the New Corporate Social Responsibility?" *Indiana University Robert H. McKinney School of Law Research Paper* 05. At http://digitalcommons.law.seattleu.edu/cgi/viewcontent.

cgi?article=2047&context=sulr (last accessed November 27, 2017).

Paniagua, Manuel. 2011. *Las empresas de la economía social. Más allá del comentario a la ley 5/2011, de economía social.* Madrid: Marcial Pons.

Paz, Narciso. 2012. *Comentario sistemático a la Ley 5/2011, de economía social.* Valencia: Tirant lo Blanch.

Sánchez, Luis Ángel, and Emilio Pérez. 2015. "Las entidades de la economía social como protagonistas de un nuevo modelo de emprendimiento y medidas legales de apoyo al emprendimiento." *CIRIEC* 84: 35–62.

Social Economy Europe. At http://www.socialeconomny.eu.org (last accessed November 27, 2017).

UK Government. 2002. *Social Enterprise: A Strategy for Success.* London: Department of Trade and Industry. At http://webarchive.nationalarchives.gov.uk/+/http://www.dti.gov.uk/socialenterprise/strat_success.htm.

———. 2011. *A Guide to Legal Forms for Social Enterprise.* London: Department for Business, Innovation & Skills. At https://www.gov.uk/government/uploads/system/uploads/attachment_data/file/31677/11-1400-guide-legal-forms-for-social-enterprise.pdf (last accessed November 27, 2017).

3

The Legal Framework of the Social Economy in the Basque Country[31]

AITOR BENGOETXEA ALKORTA

In the present work I have sought to set out the legal framework of the social economy in the Basque Country, in terms of the diverse legal spaces that concur within the European, French, Spanish, and Basque legislative areas.

The objective was to analyze the normative powers held in this area by the Basque public authorities, depending on the concrete situation of the various territories that make up the Basque Country. A distinction is made here between the case of the Northern Basque Country (Lapurdi, Zuberoa, and Behe Nafarroa); and that of the Southern Basque Country, with different legal systems for the Autonomous Community of Navarre (ACN), and for the Autonomous Community of the Basque Country (ACBC), which includes the provinces of Araba, Bizkaia, and Gipuzkoa.

---

31 Activity conducted within the framework of the Gizarte Ekonomia eta bere Zuzenbidea (Social economy and its law) research group, GIU17/052, attached to the GEZKI Institute, University of the Basque Country (UPV/EHU).

From this starting point, the criterion followed to select the regulation was clear: the regulation applicable in the Basque Country.

The object of analysis was the social economy in general, as well as the legal framework applicable to each of the entities that comprise it, as defined in the catalogue produced by the joint study of the basic norms governing the social economy in France and Spain: cooperatives; mutual associations and mutual societies; associations; foundations; worker-owned companies; insertion companies; special employment centers; agricultural processing companies; and fishermen's guilds.

The study begins with the Community Regulation on the European Cooperative Society (ECS), the only norm applicable to the whole of the Basque Country. Then, the Spanish regulation is set out in each case, in either the ACBC or the ACN, as appropriate.

In all the cases, for reasons of methodology and space, the analysis does not go beyond the basic legal concept for the social economy, in general, as well as for each particular entity that comprises it.

The case of cooperatives, around which the very concept of the social economy revolves, warrants a specific mention; it is also the only case in which the ACN and the ACBC each have their own law. The deep-rooted tradition and current vigor of the Basque cooperative movement, a world reference in this field, must have something to do with this circumstance.

In short, this study intends to set out the legal framework for the social economy and its entities within the Basque Country, identifying the regulatory channel that must be followed by social economy initiatives that are developed in our territory.

Distribution of Competences in the Social Economy Area in the Basque Country

To analyze the legal competences in the Basque Country that regulate the social economy, we must necessarily begin with explaining the present situation of division in our country.

In the Northern Basque Country, the Basque authorities as such were suppressed in the wave of standardization that followed the French Revolution. After a prolonged absence lasting over two hundred years, on January 1, 2017 a new public body, the Conurbation of the Basque Country (Communauté d'Agglomération du Pays Basque), was established. This body encompasses all the Northern Basque Country, representing the three historic territories: Lapurdi, Zuberoa, and Behe Nafarroa.

In the context of this work on the legal framework of the social economy, it must be pointed out that the new conurbation possesses competences in terms of political action for the promotion of economic development, but the Northern Basque Country does not have legislative competence of its own vis-à-vis the social economy. Consequently, where the Northern Basque Country is concerned, we will study the French legislation, as this is the legal framework that is currently applicable there.

In the Southern Basque Country, the question, from the perspective of the distribution of competences, is far more complex. The Spanish state set up autonomous communities in the Constitution of 1978 (EC), and divided the Southern Basque Country into two such bodies: the Autonomous Community of Navarre (Nafarroa), and the Autonomous Community of the Basque Community (Araba, Bizkaia, and Gipuzkoa).

In the social economy area, we find the principal reference in art. 149.1.13 of the EC, when it attributes to the Spanish state exclusive jurisdiction over the bases for and coordination of the general planning of economic activity. In line with the foregoing, art. 148.1.13 of the constitutional text itself enabled autonomous communities to take on competences promoting their own economic development within the objectives set by the economic policy of the state.

Therefore, in the generic area of the social economy, the basic legislation and coordination corresponds to the state; meanwhile, the autonomous communities can enact their own social economy legislation, as long as it falls within the state framework, and develops the basic state legislation.

Making use of that constitutional empowerment, the autonomy statute of the Basque Country assumed, as the exclusive competence of the ACBC, the promotion, economic development, and planning of the economic activity of the Basque Country in line with the general planning of the economy.[32] In the same regard, the Autonomous Community of Navarre has taken on, as its exclusive competence, and in line with the bases and development of general economic activity, the planning of economic activity, and promotion of economic development within Navarre.[33]

In consequence, the distribution of competences in the social economy area is, broadly speaking, clear: the state reserves authority for the bases and coordination, and the ACBC and ACN have exclusive competence, within the framework of the foundations laid down by the state and through their development, for the regulation of economic activity in their respective territories.

Today, then, Law 5/2011 of March 29 on the Social Economy must be considered as a basic state regulation in the social economy area.

Following the path of this law's stipulations, the entities that comprise the social economy sector are the following: cooperatives; mutual societies; foundations and associations that conduct economic activity; worker-owned companies; insertion companies; special employment centers; fishermen's guilds; and agricultural processing companies.

32 Art. 10.25 of Organic Law 3/1979, of December 18, on the Statute of Autonomy for the Basque Country (Estatuto de Autonomía del País Vasco, EAPV).
33 Art. 56 de la Law 13/1982, of August 10, on the reintegration and enhancement of the Foral Regime of Navarre (Ley Orgánica de Reintegración y Amejoramiento del Régimen Foral de Navarra, LORAFNA).

If we run through the distribution of competences in each of the concrete entities that make up the social economy family, we can observe that the ACBC and the ACN have adopted exclusive competence over cooperatives;[34] mutual societies;[35] associations;[36] and foundations.[37] In addition, the ACBC has assumed exclusive competence for fishermen's guilds.[38] Accordingly, it can develop its own legislation in these areas.

The juridical planning of worker-owned companies, insertion companies, special employment centers, and agricultural processing companies lies outside the competences of the ACN and ACBC and remains in the hands of the state.

The Framework of the European Union

In the European framework, beyond some frustrated initiatives,[39] the only regulatory standard promulgated in the social economy area has been the regulation governing the European Cooperative Society (ECS), which came into force on August 21, 2003, though its actual application was deferred until August 18, 2006.[40] Subsequently, this regulation would be complemented by a directive regarding the involvement of workers.[41]

---

34 Art. 44.27 LORAFNA; art. 10.23 EAPV.
35 Art. 44.27 LORAFNA; art. 10.23 EAPV.
36 Art. 44.19 LORAFNA; art. 10.13 EAPV.
37 Art. 44.20 LORAFNA; art. 10.13 EAPV.
38 Art. 10.21 EAPV.
39 Draft Statute for a European mutual society, the first proposal for which was reflected in (COM(1991)0273); Draft Statute for a European association, the original proposal for which can be found in DO C99, of 21.4.1992; Draft Statute for the European foundation, proposed in COM/2012/035 final - 2012/0022 (APP).
40 Regulation (EC) no. 1435/2003 of the Council, of July 22, 2003, concerning the Statute for a European cooperative society.
41 Directive 2003/72/EC of the Council, of July 22, 2003, completing the Statute for a European cooperative society in which the involvement of workers is concerned. This guarantees that there is information, consultation, participation, or another mechanism, on a transnational level, whereby workers' representatives can influence decisions that are adopted in cooperative enterprises.

Significantly, the ECS regulation specifically recognizes that the previously approved European Company regulation [42] does not adapt to the specific characteristics of cooperatives. The same assessment is made for the European Economic Interest Grouping (EEIG),[43] in that it does not satisfy the specific needs of cooperatives.

The ECS regulation notes that a cooperative is an entity recognized in the internal legislations of all the EU member states that have adopted it. It highlights as characteristics of the cooperative the fact that it is comprised of a grouping of people, with a model of democratic management, in which the primacy of people prevails, and there is an equitable distribution of the profits. The objective of the ECS centers around satisfaction of the members' needs. In the case of dissolution, any reserves will be allocated to other cooperative entities.

The function of the ECS, endowed with its own legal personality, is to encourage and enable the transnational activity of cooperatives, at the EU level. The natural or legal persons that constitute it are required to have their abode, or legal regulation, in at least two member states. The registered office of the ECS must be in the same member state as its central administration.

The ECS legal system is regulated to a great degree by the cooperative law of the member state in which the ECS has established its registered office. This explains the statement that "in fact, there is not a single European cooperative but 28 ECSs, equivalent to the number of Member States" (Fici 2014, 27).

The ECS must be registered in the member state in which it has its registered office, and in the register designated by the law of that state. The ECS acquires its legal personality on the day that it is entered in that register.

The minimum amount of capital for setting up an ECS is set at 30,000 euros. The sovereign body of the ECS is its general assembly, inherited from the classical democratic cooperative principle of "one

---

42 Regulation (EC) no. 2157/ 2001.
43 Regulation (EEC) no. 2137/85 of the Council.

person, one vote." It is also established that there is an obligation to build up statutory indivisible reserves.

In a context in which the utilization of the ECS formula has been rather limited, it is interesting to see that in the Basque Country it has constituted the legal form employed for the *ikastola* movement. *Ikastolas* are primary and secondary schools that originally emerged due to popular initiative, in the restrictive atmosphere of the Franco regime, devoted to the construction of a homegrown Basque educational model in which education is imparted in the Basque language, from and for the Basque Country.

Thus, in 2009, both the *ikastolas* in the Southern Basque Country (Araba, Bizkaia, Gipuzkoa, and Nafarroa) and their counterparts in the Northern Basque Country (Behe Nafarroa, Lapurdi, and Zuberoa) were set up as ECSs, under the designation of Euskal Herriko Ikastolak Europar Kooperatiba Elkartea (the European cooperative association of *ikastolas* of the Basque Country).

The Framework of the French State

The main reference for the social economy in French law is clearly provided by Law no. 2014-856, of July 31, covering the social and solidarity-based economy.

This law understands the sector that comprises the social and solidarity-based economy in a comprehensive way, and possible in all the realms of human economic activity, around activities of production, processing, distribution, exchange, or consumption of goods or services.

What defines this sector, as a specific economic business model, is that its development must exhibit the following characteristics:

- That its aim should not be the mere sharing out of profits.

- Democratic governance. That the participation of the various agents involved in the development of

the enterprise should not be measured in proportion
to their contribution to the cooperative's capital.

- Management will be in line with
  the following principles:

  - The profits are principally allocated
    to the aim of maintaining or develop-
    ing the activity of the enterprise.

  - The statutory reserves are indivisible.

From the technical legal perspective, entities that engage in the
activities of the social and solidarity-based economy may assume the
following legal form: cooperatives; mutual societies; associations;
foundations; and trading companies that respect the principles of
the social and solidarity-based economy that Law 2014-856 itself
defines.

Thus, we find an open clause that permits the incorporation in
the social economy of any conventional enterprise that meets the
principles of this singular economic sector.

In addition, French law includes four variants that are typical
of the European social economy, and coincide with the four cases
mentioned above, the first of which is included in the European
regulation, while the other three are present in projects that have
not yet seen the light of day: cooperatives, mutual societies, associations, and foundations.

Cooperatives were regulated in French law, more than seventy
years ago, through Law no. 47-1775, of September 10, 1947, on the
Cooperation Statute. A cooperative is defined as a company formed
by various people who have come together of their own free will to
satisfy their economic and social needs through their joint effort.

Cooperative activity must be guided by the following five principles, in agreement with five of the seven principles laid down by
the International Cooperative Alliance (ICA): voluntary membership
that is open to all (1st ICA principle); democratic governance (2nd
ICA principle); economic participation from their members (3rd

ICA principle); the training of those members (5th ICA principle); and intercooperation (6th ICA principle).[44]

Mutual societies are regulated by means of Ordinance no. 2001-350, of April 19, 2001, on the Mutual Society Code. They are non-profit private legal entities, dedicated basically to insurance activity. They carry out, through the paid contributions of their members, and in the interest of the latter and of their successors, solidarity action and mutual assistance. This law likewise provides for unions, which are second-level entities, created by mutual societies or by other unions.[45] Alongside mutual societies, Law 2014-856 covers mutual insurance companies, regulated under the Insurance Code.[46]

An association is defined in French law as an agreement whereby two or more individuals permanently bring together their knowledge or activity for a purpose other than that of sharing their gains.[47] This means that an association is characterized by its nonprofit objective.

A foundation, meanwhile, is an act whereby one or more natural or legal individuals decide on the irrevocable allocation of goods, rights, or resources to execute another nonprofit work of general interest.[48]

The Framework of the Spanish State

The framework law in this area is to be found in Law 5/2011, of March 29, on the Social Economy. This law refers to the social economy as all the economic and business activities that entities conduct in the private domain, in accordance with social economy principles, pursuing the collective interest of their members, whether that be the general economic or social interest, or both.

---

44 The ICA principles were established in 1995, and the French Law goes back to 1947, which may explain why the principles of autonomy and independence (4th ICA principle), and of concern for the community (7th ICA principle) are not specifically named.

45 A union is a concept expressly envisaged in Law 2014-856.

46 They came into being with Decree no. 76-667 of July 16, 1976.

47 Law of July 1, 1901, concerning contract of association.

48 Art. 18 of Law No. 87-571 of July 23, 1987 on the development of patronage.

The principles mentioned run as follows:

- Primacy of people and of the social purpose over capital, which is reflected in autonomous, transparent, democratic, and participatory management, leading to the prioritization of decision-making based more on people and their contributions of work and services rendered to the entity or on social purpose, than in terms of their contributions to social capital.

- Application of the results obtained from economic activity mainly in terms of work and service contributed or activity performed by associates or by members and, where appropriate, of the social purpose pursued by the entity.

- Promotion of internal and society-based solidarity to drive a commitment to local development, equal opportunities between men and women, social cohesion, integration of people at risk of social exclusion, the generation of stable, quality employment, the reconciliation of personal and family life with work, and sustainability.

- Independence vis-à-vis the public authorities.

Thus, the law includes the following entities in the social economy family: cooperatives, mutual societies, foundations and associations that conduct economic activity, worker-owned companies, insertion companies, special employment centers, fishermen's guilds, and agricultural processing companies.[49]

Here follows an outline of the legal concept regulating each of them, excepting cooperatives and fishermen's guilds, because specific regulation exists for these entities in the Southern Basque Country's legislation.

---

49 The list is open, because it concludes with a generic mention of any other entity governed by specific regulations that observe the principles of the social economy.

Where mutual societies, foundations, and associations are concerned, we saw above that both the ACN and ACBC have taken on exclusive competence over these three organizations, in their respective statutes of autonomy. In the development of these statutory provisions, specific regulations are provided for these entities today in the ACBC, but not in the ACN, which has not employed its regulatory capacity in these three areas.

Accordingly, we will analyze the Spanish regulation for these three entities because it is applicable in the ACN, while that is not the case in the ACBC.

A point to be made about mutual societies is that it must be understood that the legislator is referring to mutual insurance companies and friendly societies, and not exclusively to the second category, although the literal wording of art. 5 of the law confines itself to the term "mutual societies" (Paz Canalejo 2012, 101–2).

Mutual insurance companies are defined as nonprofit trading companies that aim to provide cover for their members, be they natural or legal persons, from risks insured via a fixed premium payable at the beginning of the risk period.[50] What characterizes these institutions, then, is their nonprofit nature, as against conventional insurance companies, which are guided by lucrative purposes.

Friendly societies also operate within the insurance field, although they function specifically on a voluntary, complementary basis with respect to the statutory social security system.[51] They are, therefore, legally defined as entities that practice a voluntary form of insurance complementary to the obligatory system, through contributions made by mutual society members, as natural or legal persons, or by other protective entities or persons.[52]

---

50 Art. 41 of Law 20/2015, of July 14, on the ordination, supervision, and solvency of insurance and reinsurance companies.

51 We must qualify that not all mutual societies act in a complementary manner vis-à-vis social security, because alternative welfare is envisaged in the case of mutual societies for professional associations (18th and 19th additional provisions of Royal Legislative Decree 8/2015, of October 30, approving the Consolidated Text of the General Social Security Law).

52 Art. 43 of Law 20/2015, of July 14, for the ordination, supervision, and solvency of insurance and reinsurance companies.

Foundations are legally constituted nonprofit organizations whose patrimony, by wish of their founders, is tied up in a lasting way with the attainment of goals of general interest.[53]

Associations, meanwhile, are established by agreement among three or more natural or legal persons who are legally constituted, to make a commitment to pool knowledge, means, and activities to achieve lawful common aims, of general or particular interest, and endow themselves with statutes that govern the association's operations.[54]

The workforce-owned company is a particular legal figure in Spanish legislation, and exists neither in comparative European law, nor in general EU law. This is a limited company or limited liability company, in which most of the social capital belongs to the workers who render services there and are rewarded personally and directly, through an employment relationship for an indefinite period. Furthermore, none of the members may possess more than a third of the social capital.[55]

A workforce-owned company, therefore, is essentially a conventional capitalist trading company, limited company, or workforce-owned company. But the fact that most of the social capital belongs to the actual people who work in the firm, place this legal construct within the social economy area, as a formula for collective self-employment.

Insertion companies are entities in which there is sheltered employment for a specific collective of working people: those who are in a situation of social exclusion. These enterprises are legally defined as legally constituted trading companies or cooperative societies that carry out any kind of economic activity involving the production of goods and services, whose social purpose is the integration and training of people in a situation of social exclusion, as a route toward

---

53 Art. 2 of Law 50/2002, of December 26, on Foundations.
54 Art. 5 of Organic Law 1/2002, March 22, regulating the Right of Association.
55 Art. 1 of Law 44/2015, of October 14, on Worker-owned and Investee Companies.

obtaining a regular job.[56] These enterprises must have personnel on their books in the process of labor insertion; during the first three years of activity they must constitute at least thirty percent of the total workforce, and from the fourth year onward this figure must have reached at least fifty percent.

Consequently, what characterizes insertion companies is not their legal form, which is that of a cooperative or a trading company, but their social purpose, which is necessarily guided by the objective of providing employment to people in a situation of social exclusion.

Special employment centers display a marked resemblance to insertion companies, although their objective is to provide sheltered employment to another disadvantaged collective: disabled people.

They are firms whose main aim is that of carrying out a productive activity involving goods or services, participating in market operations on a regular basis, and they are intended to ensure gainful employment for people with disabilities; at the same time, they act as a means of including the greatest number of such people on ordinary employment contracts.[57] A minimum of 70 percent of those on the payroll in special employment centers must be disabled people.

Special employment centers may be under public or private ownership and may be profit or nonprofit organizations. What determines their inclusion in the social economy area is the social function of these enterprises, favoring the employment of those with disabilities.

Lastly, agricultural processing companies are civil societies with an economic-social purpose associated with the production, processing, and marketing of agricultural, livestock, or forestry products, the execution of improvements in rural areas, agricultural promotion and development and the provision of common services that assist

---

56 Art. 4 of Law 44/2007, of December 13, for the regulation of the insertion company system.

57 Art. 43 of Royal Legislative Decree 1/2013, of November 29, approving the Consolidated Text of the General Law governing the rights of persons with disabilities, and their social inclusion.

that purpose.[58] These entities perform their activity in the field of agriculture, in line with the principles of the social economy.

The Basque Framework

In this section we examine the five legal figures that have been regulated by the legislation of the ACN (cooperatives); and by legislation in the ACBC (cooperatives, mutual societies, associations, foundations, and fishermen's guilds).

We begin with Navarrese law, which defines a cooperative as a company that, complying in its organization and operation with the principles formulated by the International Cooperative Alliance in the terms laid down in the Foral Law of Navarre, performs, as a joint undertaking, any economic-social activity at the service of its members and in the interest of the community.[59]

Navarrese law, therefore, and rightly so, in my opinion, relates the list of characteristics that cooperatives must meet to the principles of the ICA; voluntary, open membership; democratic control by the membership; economic participation from members; autonomy and independence; education, training, and information; intercooperation; and concern for the community (International Cooperative Alliance, 1995).

The longer-standing law governing cooperatives in the ACBC, meanwhile, characterizes a cooperative as a company that develops an enterprise whose prime aim is the promotion of the economic and social activities of its members and satisfaction of their needs with their active participation, observing the principles of the cooperative movement and serving the surrounding community.[60]

In the case of the ACBC, although the ICA is not specifically mentioned, we must naturally understand that the cooperative

---

58 Art. 1 of Royal Decree 1776/1981, of August 3, approving the statute that regulates agricultural processing companies.

59 Art. 2 of Foral Law 14/2006, of December 11, on Cooperatives in Navarre.

60 Art. 1 of Law 4/1993, of June 24, on Cooperatives in the Basque Country.

principles to be met are those that are listed by this body, which represents the worldwide cooperative movement.

Mutual societies, for their part, are defined as voluntary social welfare entities, whose purpose is to perform social welfare that is voluntary or complementary to the social welfare system, within the confines of the ACBC.[61]

Among the main principles that inform the activity of these insurance entities, in contrast with others that operate in the market, are the absence of a profit motive, and the democratic structure and composition of their governing bodies. This includes them within the social economy area.

Foundations, meanwhile, in the ACBC regulation, are defined as nonprofit organizations whose patrimony, by wish of its founders, is tied up in a lasting way with the attainment of goals of general interest.[62]

Associations, proceeding from the assumption that everyone has a right to associate freely to achieve licit ends, are characterized as nonprofit private entities based on people, organized to accomplish particular or general purposes.[63]

Lastly, fishermen's guilds are defined as public law corporations endowed with a legal personality and the capacity to act in pursuit of their purposes, which are legally instituted as a participatory channel collaborating with the fishing sector alongside the public administrations in defense of the general interest of fishing, shellfish harvesting, and aquaculture, and of the organization and marketing of their products.[64]

The fact that fishermen's guilds are public law corporations, included in the social economy area by the law on social economy, is particularly striking, given that the law itself explicitly expresses that the social economy is developed within the private domain.

---

61 Art. 1 of Law 5/2012, of February 23, on Voluntary Social Welfare Entities.
62 Art. 2 of Law 9/2016, of June 2, on Foundations in the Basque Country.
63 Art. 3 of Law 7/2007, of June 22, on Associations in the Basque Country.
64 Art. 1 of Law 16/1998, of June 25, on Fishermen's Guilds.

There seems to be an obvious contradiction.[65] Furthermore, there is a hurdle that is hard for a public law corporation to clear, constituted by the necessary independence of social economy entities vis-à-vis the public authorities, in the shape of the fourth ICA principle that the law on social economy also specifically establishes.

Conclusion

Throughout the study I have endeavored to demarcate the complex framework of the public authorities' legal powers in the Basque Country where the social economy area is concerned.

In the Northern Basque Country, due to the lack of legislative competence in this field of the Conurbation of the Basque Country, the public institution that covers its three historic territories, we studied the French legislation.

This legislation has a framework law that encompasses the entire social and solidarity-based economy, while also providing specific regulations for cooperatives, mutual societies, associations, and foundations. In the French legislation we found, *mutatis mutandis*, universally accepted concepts on the social economy in general, and regarding legal entities that include cooperatives, mutual societies, associations, and foundations. This is the framework that permits and encourages the development of social economy initiatives in the Southern Basque Country.

In the context of the Northern Basque Country, I explained the system of distribution of competences configured by the Spanish constitution, and the statutes of autonomy of the Autonomous Community of Navarre and of the Autonomous Community of the Basque Country.

In current positive law, we must turn to the state legislation when we want to develop business initiatives in the Southern Basque

---

65 There is specialized doctrine on this issue that supports their inclusion in the social economy area, given that they meet its principles, as pointed out by Botana Agra and Millán Calenti (2016).

Country involving worker-owned companies, special employment centers, insertion companies, or agricultural processing companies.

Meanwhile, the ACBC has its own regulations governing cooperatives, mutual societies, associations, foundations, and fishermen's guilds. The ACN possesses its own standards regulating cooperatives in Navarre, while state law is applied to the remaining social economy entities.

Aside from the distribution of competences, if we consider the substantive regulation when the different legal systems are compared (European, French, Spanish, and Basque), we find no substantial differences in the regulation of the social economy sector, in general, nor in the various entities that comprise it. These are institutions with a great tradition behind them, and with reasonably consolidated characteristics, which is why the substantive legislation does not markedly differ.

However, to nuance this general assertion, we should dwell on the specific case of cooperatives. They stand as the core social economy family institution, with the greatest socioeconomic potential, even as a lever for social transformation, given that their approach posits an economic system in terms of cooperation, attempting to overcome the classic conflict between capital and work.

Cooperatives as entities are the object of the most varied legal-positive regulation. It is the only regulated entity in European law, as well as the only regulated entity in Navarrese law. It is, likewise, the only social economy figure that produces a specific legal framework within the Basque context, in the respective norms of the ACBC and of the ACN.

Therefore, although the perspective of this study is to set out the legal framework of the social economy, with only a scarce examination of aspects of content, a deeper look is warranted in the case of cooperatives.

The legal regulation of cooperatives, beyond the lowest common denominator that we can find in the universal principles, defined so well by the ICA, has broad room for maneuver, when elucidating a diversity of far-reaching issues.

Thus, in the case of associated work cooperatives, the ACN and ACBC regulations can choose between various degrees of self-management in the labor conditions of member-workers. Navarrese law has now opted for pure self-management, leaving out references to labor law. The law in the ACBC is almost the same, the only conditioning factor being the minimum interprofessional salary. In comparative cooperative law, diametrically opposite models exist, such as the law on cooperatives in Extremadura, which establishes the application of labor law, en bloc, for cooperative worker-members.

In many other aspects of the cooperative legal system, various important options are also provided for, such as cases in which a minimum number of people is stipulated to be able to set up a cooperative; there is a minimum amount of capital; there are windows for action for members who contribute only capital; there is an allowance of wage labor in cooperatives; different approaches to taxation are covered; there is an economic regime involving reserve funds; a system of attribution of losses to worker members exists; and the list goes on.

To sum up, one can conclude by underlining that, beyond the essential, universal characteristics of the social economy and of the entities that make it up, the regulations proper to the ACN and to the ACBC provide the juridical design of the legal-cooperative system with wide room for maneuver.

Bibliography

Askunze Elizaga, Carlos. 2016. "Empresas de inserción en la economía social. Herramientas para la inclusión sociolaboral." *CIRIEC-España: Revista jurídica de economía social y cooperativa* 29: 15–46.

Bengoetxea Alkorta, Aitor. 2016. "Las cooperativas." *CIRIEC-España: Revista jurídica de economía social y cooperativa* 29: 205–34.

Botana Agra, Manuel José, and Rafael Álvaro Millán Calenti. 2016. "Cofradías de pescadores." *CIRIEC-España: Revista jurídica de economía social y cooperativa* 29: 117–46.

Del Burgo García, Unai. 2013. "El movimiento cooperativo de las ikastolas: su revisión conceptual desde la perspectiva de las empresas sociales." *Revista Vasca de economía social: GEZKI* 10: 71–96.

Díaz-Aguado Jalón, Carlos. 2016. "Las asociaciones." *CIRIEC-España: Revista jurídica de economía social y cooperativa* 29: 81–116.

Domínguez Cabrera, María del Pino. 2016. "Los principios de la Economía Social en la Ley de Sociedades Laborales y Participadas." *CIRIEC-España: Revista jurídica de economía social y cooperativa* 29: 185–204.

Fici, Antonio. 2014. "La sociedad cooperativa europea: cuestiones y perspectivas." *CIRIEC-España: Revista jurídica de economía social y cooperativa* 25: 1–54.

Mauleón Méndez, Emilio, and Juana Isabel Genovart Balaguer. 2016. "La inclusión de la sociedad agraria de transformación en la Ley de Economía Social. Pretensión del legislador o realidad en la praxis empresarial." *CIRIEC-España: Revista jurídica de economía social y cooperativa* 29: 147–84.

Montero Vilar, José Antonio, Cristina Pedrosa Leis, and Mª Cristina Reza Conde. 2016. "Mutualidades de previsión social, economía social y mercado asegurador." *CIRIEC-España: Revista jurídica de economía social y cooperativa* 29: 47–79.

Moratalla Santamaría, Pablo. 2016. "Centros Especiales de Empleo." *CIRIEC-España: Revista jurídica de economía social y cooperativa* 29: 235–72.

Paniagua Zurera, Manuel. 2011. *Las empresas de la economía social. Más allá del Comentario a la Ley 5/2011, de Economía Social*. Madrid: Marcial Pons.

Paz Canalejo, Narciso. 2012. *Comentario sistemático a la Ley 5/2011, de Economía Social*. Valencia: Tirant lo Blanch.

Normative Appendix

Council Regulation (EC) no. 1435/2003, of July 22, 2003, concerning the Statute for a European cooperative society.

French Constitution (1958).

Law no. 2014-856, of July 31, concerning the Social and Solidarity Economy.

Law no. 47-1775, of September 10, 1947, concerning the Cooperation Statute.

Ordinance no. 2001-350, of April 19, 2001, on the Mutual Society Code.

Decree no. 76-667, of July 16, 1976, on the Insurance Code.

Law no. 2003-709 of August 1, 2003, concerning patronage, associations, and foundations.

Law of July 1, 1901, concerning contract of association.

Law no. 87-571, of July 23, 1987, on the development of patronage.

Spanish Constitution (1978).

Law 5/2011, of March 29, on Social Economy.

Law 20/2015, of July 14, on the ordination, supervision, and solvency of insurance and reinsurance companies.

Law 50/2002, of December 26, on Foundations.

Organic Law 1/2002, of March 22, regulating the Right of Association.

Law 44/2015, of October 14, on Worker-owned, and Investee Companies.

Law 44/2007, of December 13, for the regulation of the insertion company system.

Royal Legislative Decree 1/2013, of November 29, approving the Consolidated Text of the General Law on the rights of people with disabilities and their social inclusion.

Royal Decree 1776/1981, of August 3, approving the Statute that regulates agricultural processing companies.

Organic Law 13/1982, of August 10, on the reintegration and enhancement of the Foral Regime of Navarre.

Foral Law 14/2006, of December 11, on Cooperatives in Navarre.

Organic Law 3/1979, of December 18, on the Autonomy Statute for the Basque Country.

Law 4/1993, of June 24, on Cooperatives in the Basque Country.

Law 5/2012, of February 23, on Voluntary Social Welfare Entities (in the ACBC)

Law 9/2016, of June 2, on Foundations in the Basque Country.

Law 7/2007, June 22, on Associations in the Basque Country.

Law 16/1998, June 25, on Fishermen's Guilds (ACBC).

4

Reality and Evolution of the Social Economy in the Autonomous Community of Euskadi

ARATZ SOTO GORROTXATEGI AND ANE ETXEBARRIA RUBIO

In this chapter we attempt to depict the current reality of the social economy sector in the Autonomous Community of Euskadi[66] (ACE), as well as its recent evolution since the turn of the century, presenting and analyzing legislation and socioeconomic data of relevance for the sector. To meet this objective, we have drawn on the daily work we carry out in the Basque Social Economy Observatory.

This work falls into three main sections. In the first there is a brief presentation of the Basque Social Economy Observatory (Observatorio Vasco de Economía Social-Gizarte Ekonomiako Euskal Behatokia, OVES/GEEB) and the working areas from which it operates. The second section analyses the evolution and situation of the social economy's most relevant families in the ACE, focusing the analysis on legislation and socioeconomic data. Lastly, the

---

66 Euskadi is a synonym for the Basque Country.

chapter closes with some concluding remarks concerning the present and future of the social economy in Araba, Bizkaia, and Gipuzkoa.

For a complete analysis of the reality in the sector, we would certainly have to take questions into account that, for reasons of space, we will not be able to deal with in depth. In this regard, the research concentrated on the most relevant families, and excluded financial entities, agricultural processing companies, and fishermen's guilds. Also excluded were all the data and regulations available on the observatory's website.[67]

The Basque Social Economy Observatory

The Basque Social Economy Observatory was established through a collaboration agreement of December 30, 2008 signed between the Basque government, represented by the Minister of Justice, Employment, and Social Welfare at the time, and the UPV/EHU (University of the Basque Country), represented by the Institute of Cooperative Law and Social Economy (Gizarte Ekonomia eta Zuzenbide Kooperatiboaren Institutua, GEZKI), for the progressive implementation of the observatory. This constituted a response to the resolutions of the Basque parliament's Work and Social Action Commission, published on April 25, 2008 in the BOPV (Boletín Oficial del País Vasco, Official Bulletin of the Basque Country, no. 153), regarding the need to establish a body with these characteristics (no. 8).[68]

The OVES/GEEB was created to encourage the development of the social economy through the identification and quantification of its activity in the Autonomous Community of Euskadi, understanding this to be to be the sector that brings together those

---

67 See www.oves-geeb.eus.

68 "The Basque parliament proposes to the public administrations that they take the leading steps necessary to arrive at the creation of a body (institute, foundation, or observatory) that draws together all the social economy actors and institutions (government, provincial, and city councils) for the permanent analysis of the state of the Basque social economy, its quantification and conjunctures, in order to deal with the problems that affect it and its immediate and future needs."

entities of a private nature whose common characteristic is that they are formed to satisfy social needs and not to provide returns to capitalist investors (Bretos 2015), as stipulated in the principles recognized in the Social Economy[69] Law 5/2011, which was passed at a later date.

Since its creation in 2008, the Basque Social Economy Observatory has received support from the Basque universities, and from actors and persons of standing in the Basque social economy.

There are, in principle, three functional areas in the OVES/GEEB:

- Socioeconomic area: capture and publication of economic, social, and work-related data for social economy organizations, and their socioeconomic environment: Employment, Entities, and economic data.

- Legal-political area: identification and analysis both of the legislation and of the general regulations current and applicable to the Basque social economy, the public policies aimed at the sector, and political initiatives originating in the different political institutions.

- Scientific-academic area: systematization of doctrinal production on the social economy, for the purposes of furnishing support to those researching the development of its activity, offering a guide of the main social economy research networks and resources.

Legislation and Evolution of the Social Economy in the Autonomous Community of Euskadi

As mentioned above, the Autonomous Community of Euskadi does not have its own law on social economy. Instead, there is a basic general norm that has the force of a law at the Spanish state level, establishing a common juridical framework for all organizations in the social economy.

---

69 https://www.boe.es/diario_boe/txt.php?id=BOE-A-2011-5708.

Social Economy[70] Law 5/2011, March 29, was the first law to define and delimit the social economy, thereby constituting recognition of the sector's reality. Its status as a basic general regulation enables and makes necessary actions undertaken by the autonomous communities to develop it through norms and public policies, without altering or exhausting the regulatory power of these administrations in this area.

The passing of the present law clearly represented progress in the legal structuring of the sector, thanks to which it acquires legal status as an active interlocutor before the public administrations. This precept neither replaces nor modifies any other regulations, because the main aim, as the document itself stipulates, is rather to establish a common juridical framework for all the entities that comprise the social economy. Additionally, for the first time it specifies which bodies make up, or might become part of, this sector (Art.5).[71]

The norm certainly stands as a key instrument for the advancement of the social economy, in that it underlines the need and obligation to promote and disseminate the sector by means of measures that foster each of its constituent entities. Article 8 is of relevance in this regard, as it establishes that promotion of the sector will be an undertaking of general interest, and that the public authorities will be obliged to promote it through the adoption of concrete measures.

This law respects the specific regulations that govern each of the social economy modalities present in the different public administrations, depending on the powers granted to them in this matter. Most autonomous communities have developed regulations and measures within the scope of their powers (Art. 3), and have

---

70 https://www.boe.es/diario_boe/txt.php?id=BOE-A-2011-5708.

71 "1. The social economy is made up of cooperatives, mutual societies, foundations, and associations that conduct economic activity, worker owned companies, insertion companies, special employment centers, fishermen's guilds, agricultural processing companies, and singular entities created by specific regulations governed by the principles established in the preceding article. 2. Likewise, organizations may form part of the social economy if they carry out economic and business activity, and their operating rules respect the principles listed in the preceding article, and they are also included in the catalogue of entities stipulated in article 6 of this law. 3. In all events, social economy entities will be governed by their specific substantive rules."

Table 4.1

	Number of entities, and of those employed in the Social Economy (non-financial institutions). 2016				Weight of the ES in the general Economy of the ACE	
	Entities	% Entity	Employ-ment	% Employ-ment	Entities	Employ-ment
Cooperatives	1,599	6.12%	57,815	64.93%	1.03%	6.77%
Worker Owned Companies	623	2.39%	6,876	7.72%	0.40%	0.81%
Special Employment Centers	13	0.05%	8,852	9.94%	0.01%	1.04%
Insertion Companies	44	0.17%	1,122	1.26%	0.03%	0.13%
Agricultural Processing Companies	94*	0.36%	239*	0.27%	0.06%	0.03%
Fishermen's Guilds	15	0.06%	68	0.08%	0.01%	0.01%
Associations and Foundations	23,728	90.86%	14,075*	15.81%	15.34%	1.65%
Total Social Economy (Non-financial)	26.116	100.00%	89,047	100.00%	16.88%	10.43%
Total Economy ACE (1)	154.687	-	854,114	-	100.00%	100.00%

*Data for 2014 Source: OVES/GEEB (1) Source: EUSTAT

already regulated the sector through the enactment of their own legislation, as Galicia[72] did, by means of Law 6/2016 governing the social economy of Galicia.

In historical terms, cooperatives and associations have had a very prominent role in the social economy sector of the ACE, either through their importance within the productive fabric of the territory, or within the nonentrepreneurial associative network. This is reflected in the following table, which also shows the current cartography of the sector.

Associations and foundations constitute the overwhelming bulk of the entities, but it must be borne in mind that many of these are nonmarket bodies and, further, it is hard to know how many of them really practice their activity (whether of an economic kind or not) on a regular basis. As for the rest, the greatest number of organizations fall into the category of cooperatives and worker owned companies, followed on a smaller scale by agricultural processing companies, insertion companies, special employment centers, and fishermen's guilds, in that order.

Turning to the employment figures, we see that the cooperatives occupy the most important position in the ACE, employing two thirds of the total employment in the social economy. The associations and foundations, for their part, also accumulate in their organizations a considerable percentage (at around 15 percent) of the overall total for jobs. Meanwhile, special employment centers certainly account for higher employment figures than other kinds of legal forms that are represented by greater numbers of entities, which is explained by the fact that various substantially large enterprises of this kind exist. It must also be noted that worker owned companies, which amount to 2.40 percent of the total number of social economy entities, employ in their enterprises almost 8 percent of the overall job total. Lastly, insertion companies currently employ over one thousand people.

---

72 Law 6/2016, May 4, on the social economy de Galicia. At https://www.boe. es/buscar/doc.php?id=BOE-A-2016-5943.

Table 4.2

Overall numbers of entities and of those employed in the Social Economy (non-financial institutions), and their evolution					
	2008		2016		Variation (%)
	Entities	Employ-ment	Entities	Employ-ment	Entities	Employ-ment
Total Social Economy	23.013	88,044	26,116	89,047	13.48%	1.14%

Source: OVES/GEEB

If we look at the relative weight of the social economy in the general economy of the three historical territories, we see that it occupies over 10 percent of the total employment. Although the sector obviously constitutes just a small part of the business fabric, by nature this economy is advancing steadily, acquiring increasing significance.

To complete the first approach to the current general cartography of the social economy, before moving on to analyze the current sociolegal reality of each family, it is useful to run through (even if superficially) the evolution that the whole sector has registered over the last years.

We see that, in general, since the crisis began in 2008, both the number of entities and of those employed in them have increased, although it is true that each family has taken its own path, as we will observe when we focus on each case. Here, it is striking that the slight rise in employment during this period, at 1.14 percent, contrasts with the massive losses experienced by the ACE's economy in general, highlighting a greater capacity for facing up to the crisis and the stronger recovery made by the social economy when compared to other entrepreneurial modalities.

Cooperatives

No one is unaware of the importance that cooperativism has had and still does in the Basque Country, and this is why the ACE's legislation for such companies has taken on such a central role and been more robustly developed by the legislators. The supreme law of the Spanish judicial order, the Constitution of 1978,[73] already expressly referred to the cooperative model in its article 129.2[74], representing recognition of such organizations and providing the foundations upon which appropriate and specific legislation could be developed.

---

73 https://www.boe.es/buscar/doc.php?id=BOE-A-1978-31229.
74 "2. The public authorities will effectively promote diverse forms of participation in the company and will foster cooperative companies, by means of adequate legislation. They will also establish the means to facilitate the workers' access to ownership of the means of production."

Cooperativism has been the exclusive responsibility of some autonomous communities, among them the ACE.[75] And they made use of article 149.3[76] of the Spanish Constitution to develop their own cooperative legislation. This has meant that today in the Spanish state some sixteen autonomous Laws[77] have been passed. In addition, there is one general cooperative law[78] that has been the subject of a legislative development never before witnessed by autonomous communities, creating a juridical reality without precedent.

In 1982 the first Basque Law on Cooperatives, Law 11/1982, February 29, was enacted, a groundbreaking move within the Spanish state. This norm revealed various deficiencies, and proved to be short lived and at times very limited, so that in cases of a legal vacuum it eventually became necessary to refer to the general law on cooperatives.[79] This situation led the legislators to pass a new broader policy, Law 4/1993, June 24, on Cooperatives in Euskadi,[80] indispensable to meeting the sector's needs.

The 1993 law is the current regulation at the time of writing, but it has been developed and reformed on several occasions, mainly because of the need to adapt to the new times and to the sector's demands. The objective of the reforms[81] carried out over recent

---

75 Such responsibility was exclusively attributed by Art. 10.23 of the Statute of Autonomy for the ACE, via the Organic Law 3/1979, December 18.

76 "3. It will be possible for matters not exclusively attributed to the state by this constitution to correspond to the autonomous communities, by virtue of their respective statutes. Competence for matters that have not been assumed by the autonomy statutes will correspond to the state, whose norms will prevail, in cases of conflict, over those of the autonomous communities in all that is not attributed to be of their exclusive competence. State law will, in all cases, be supplementary to the law applicable in the autonomous communities."

77 Andalusia, Aragón, Asturias, Balearics, Cantabria, Castile La Mancha, Castile and León, Catalonia, Extremadura, Galicia, La Rioja, Madrid, Murcia, Navarre, the Basque Country, and Valencia.

78 https://www.boe.es/buscar/act.php?id=BOE-A-1999-15681.

79 General Law on Cooperatives 3/1987, April 2.

80 https://www.boe.es/buscar/pdf/2012/BOE-A-2012-2011-consolidado.pdf.

81 Particularly noteworthy are Law 1/2000, June 29, modifying the LGC (Ley General de Cooperativas, General Law on Cooperatives); Law 8/2006, December 1, the second modification of the LGC; Law 6/2008, June 25, on Small Cooperative Companies in Euskadi.

years has been to adjust to the requirements demanded by the new norms stemming from European and international institutions and modifications in state legislation or in other autonomous regions. In addition, various decrees[82] and regulations have been passed addressed at developing the principal rule, including the promotion of cooperativism and training in that area for young entrepreneurs.

The Basque regulation of cooperatives has been and continues to be in a state of constant evolution and permanent change and the Basque government is currently (summer of 2018) working on a new Basque cooperative law, the legislative bill for which will be presented before the Basque parliament in the second half of 2018. For the development of this new regulation, the executive has created a work group with concerned associations and cooperative bodies to prepare a diagnostic study of the sector and agree on the future law.

The new legislative project does not replace the basic structure of the current law, but seeks to combine, in a single text, the different modifications that have been introduced since the regulation of 1993 was enacted. The legislator's aim is to provide greater legal certainty to the sector's internal and external relations and improve its internal organizational system.

The cooperative sector has, in general, had a very positive evolution since the turn of the twenty-first century, given that, except for the unrelenting setbacks received due to the crisis (initially in 2008 with the first downturn, and then between 2012 and 2014), the number of entities and of people employed has increased steadily from year to year. In this regard, since the start of the century, employment in cooperatives has risen roughly to the tune of 29 percent. Between 2016 and 2018, 2016 stands out for the greatest year-on-year growth of entities since the crisis began

---

82 Decree 58/2005 endorsing the regulation implementing the Basque Law on Cooperatives; Decree 59/2005, which endorses the regulations on the organization and functioning of the RCE (Registro de Cooperativas de Euskadi, Register of Cooperative Societies in the Basque Country); Decree 61/2000, which regulates social initiative cooperatives; regulation on conflict resolution.

Table 4.3

Evolution of the number of Cooperatives and of people employed in the ACE. 2000-2016								
Year	**2000**	**2001**	**2002**	**2003**	**2004**	**2005**	**2006**	**2007**
Entities	1,331	1,350	1,383	1,403	1,443	1,471	1,466	1,491
People employed	44,970	48,799	50,835	52,271	54,038	55,438	56,738	58,238

	2008
	1,511
	55,507

Year	**2009**	**2010**	**2011**	**2012**	**2013**	**2014**	**2015**	**2016**
Entities	1,478	1,498	1,522	1,533	1,536	1,532	1,555	1,599
People employed	55,121	56,231	57,122	56,365	56,251	55,958	56,380	57,815

Source: OVES/GEEB

(2.83 percent). Furthermore, that same year, the figure for people employed in cooperatives in the ACE rose by 2.55 percent, coming close to the historic high ever recorded (in 2007) and exceeding the level of employment in 2008.

Turning to gender now, we only have the aggregated statistic for cooperatives and worker owned companies, showing that 47.2 percent of the total employment in these entities is occupied by women, against 52.8 percent of jobs held by men.

Worker Owned Companies

Worker owned companies both in the past and today represent a significant part of the economic fabric in the ACE. This company model has a long track record, and acquired the seal of legal status in 1986 with the enactment of Law 15/1986, April 25, on Public Limited Labor Companies,[83] the first legislation at state level to regulate this model, including all the characteristics that had defined such companies over time. This law was enacted in response to the mandate of article 129.2 of the Spanish Constitution, which states that the authorities must effectively promote the different types of participation in enterprises and establish the means whereby working people can be provided access to the ownership of the means of production.

The first regulation proved, as time passed, to be insufficient, and was repealed by Law 4/1997, on Worker Owned Companies,[84] which remained in force until 2015. Its greatest potential lay in the extension of the worker owned company to the status of a limited liability company.[85]

Faced with deficiencies in the law and the need to adapt to new legislative scenarios and social and economic reality, the sector called for a new reform to reinforce the essential features of

---

83 https://www.boe.es/buscar/doc.php?id=BOE-A-1986-10626.

84 https://www.boe.es/buscar/doc.php?id=BOE-A-1997-6258.

85 Spurred by the reform of company law initiated by Law 19/1989, July 25, which partially reformed and adapted commercial legislation to EEC directives on companies, giving a decisive boost to limited liability companies.

this company model. This situation led the legislative branch to prepare the new Law 44/2015, on Worker Owned and Investee Companies,[86] which for the first time includes the modality of the investee company. This legislation, as the text itself declares, aims to adapt the legal system of worker owned companies to the reforms that have taken place in recent years and, further, foster participation from working people, increase these companies' preference for entrepreneurship, and facilitate the setting up of this type of company, among other objectives.

One of the most significant innovations of the new norm is the incorporation of the investee company model for working people, which had not until that time been regulated in Spain, and the legislator in this case deemed it appropriate to do so within the framework of the law on worker owned companies. As the actual legislation defines it, these are investee companies, public limited, or limited liability companies that do not meet the requirements set for them to be classified as such, but promote workers' access to worker membership status, and to the different forms of participation.[87]

For worker owned companies the decade following the outbreak of the global economic crisis was quite bleak when compared with the general dynamic the social economy has followed. Observing the data, we see that the crisis marked a watershed in the development of these entities, for two clearly separated stages can be distinguished on each side of the divide. In the first stage (2000–2007), both the number of entities and of people employed remained relatively constant and at levels that are far from negligible. In contrast, from 2008 onward there was an important regression in the worker owned companies, above all in the employment figures, because in six years half of the jobs were lost. However, one should also bear in mind that, between 2014 and 2016, there was an unusual trend in that while the number of these entities continues to diminish, their employment figures rose. This underscores the fact that the worker owned companies that are still operationally

---

86 https://www.boe.es/diario_boe/txt.php?id=BOE-A-2015-11071.
87 Article 19 of Law 44/2015 on Worker Owned and Investee Companies.

Table 4.4 Evolution in the number of Worker Owned Companies and people employed in the ACE. 2000-2016

Year	2000	2001	2002	2003	2004	2005	2006	2007	2008
Entities	1,003	1,049	1,121	1,146	1,124	1,103	1,062	1,023	931
People employed	13,146	12,759	12,930	13,036	12,510	13,356	13,693	13,561	12,565

Year	2009	2010	2011	2012	2013	2014	2015	2016
Entities	864	815	762	709	674	659	644	623
People employed	11,444	9,177	7,945	7,275	6,519	6,679	6,758	6,876

Source: OVES/GEEB

active in the ACE are demonstrating a solid business structure, as they are proving capable of generating a rising number of jobs, while the number of enterprises continues to decrease.

Special Employment Centers

Special employment centers (SECs) are institutions that work to achieve a more sustainable economy and a more cohesive society, prioritizing improvements in the labor and social integration of people with diverse abilities (Moratalla 2015, 74). They also share the fundamental principles of the social economy and that is why, in 2011, with the passing of Law 5/2011, they became yet one more family in the social economy.[88]

For an analysis of their regulatory development, we must go back to 1982, when Law 13/1982, April 7, was passed, dealing with the social integration of disabled persons(Ley de Integración Social de los Minusválidos, LISMI),[89] which has been the reference standard for this collective. Years later, Law 51/2003, December 2, was adopted, covering equal opportunities, nondiscrimination, and the universal accessibility of people with disabilities,[90] contributing new impetus in the struggle against discrimination. It is worth pointing to Law 49/2007,[91] which set up a system of infringements and penalties in the field of equal opportunities, nondiscrimination, and the universal accessibility of this collective.

All these laws were repealed by Law 26/2011,[92] following ratification by Spain in 2007 of the United Nations General Assembly's International Convention on the Rights of People with Disabilities, thereby making it necessary to adapt the regulations in line with that convention. In consequence, the Royal Legislative Decree 1/2013 was passed, with a rewriting of the text of the general law on the rights

---

88 Art. 5 of Law 5/2011, on the Social Economy.
89 https://www.boe.es/buscar/doc.php?id=BOE-A-1982-9983.
90 https://www.boe.es/buscar/act.php?id=BOE-A-2003-22066.
91 https://www.boe.es/buscar/act.php?id=BOE-A-2007-22293.
92 https://www.boe.es/buscar/act.php?id=BOE-A-2011-13241.

of people with disabilities and their social inclusion.[93] This legislation currently legally defines (Art. 43) and regulates the special employment centers. In addition to this standard, other regulatory references are maintained, among them, Royal Decree 2273/1985, December 4,[94] which governs some fundamental aspects and defines some of the most important characteristics of the SECs.

Meanwhile, organizations representing special social initiative employment centers (known as CEEIS, Centros Especiales de Empleo de Iniciativa Social)[95] demanded the reform of Law 5/2011, on the Social Economy. Article 5 of the precept recognizes as social economy institutions all special employment centers, but the reality is that there is a diversity of entities in the sector pursuing interests, objectives, and extremely heterogeneous purposes, which in many cases do not adopt or act upon the principles and objectives that the social economy promotes. That is what motivated the CEEIS to propose a revision and updating of this law, adapting article 5 to the sector's reality, and that, in relation to the protected employment sector, only special social initiative employment centers be included, because these entities share and implement (according to the organizations representing the CEEIS) the principles, values, and objectives of the social economy.

The socioeconomic evolution of the special employment centers since 2008 has been remarkable, especially where the number of people employed is concerned. In this period the personnel in these institutions has grown by almost 36 percent and, despite the adverse economic situation, absolute employment losses have only been recorded for two years (in 2009 and 2012). What is really striking about the data for SECs is that, thanks to what has been called the "Basque model of inclusion," currently around 85 percent of the

---

93 https://www.boe.es/buscar/doc.php?id=BOE-A-2013-12632.
94 https://www.boe.es/buscar/doc.php?id=BOE-A-1985-25591.
95 They are promoted by social and third sector entities, pioneers in the generation of employment for disabled people using the protected employment formula, especially for the collective of disabled people with greater needs of support, including those with an intellectual disability, mental illness, and physical and sensorial disability with a degree of disability equal to or higher than 65 percent.

Table 4.5

Evolution of the number of Special Employment Centers and of people employed in the ACE. 2000-2016										
Year	2007	2008	2009	2010	2011	2012	2013	2014	2015	2016
Entities	6	6	6	6	8	9	11	12	13	13
People employed	6,468	6,485	6,356	6,654	6,858	6,786	7,231	7,746	7,961	8,789
Permanent wage-earners	65.1%	69.8%	71.9%	69.0%	673%	68.6%	68.5%	64.4%	61.9%	62.4%
Women	38.3%	38.2%	38.6%	38.0%	35.9%	36.7%	37.5%	45.5%	38.2%	40.6%
Disabled persons	83.1%	83.5%	83.3%	83.8%	86.0%	86.4%	86.5%	85.8%	90.4%	85.1%

Source: OVES/GEEB

people working in SECs are disabled in some way, not forgetting that a policy of promoting the transfer of these people to "ordinary employment" is in place, and is also registering increases. An examination of the contractual relation of workers shows that the evolution has taken the shape of an inverted "u" because, while the tendency during the early years was for the percentage of people on permanent contracts to rise, following the high point in 2009 (72 percent permanent vs 28 percent temporary), a decrease in the proportion of permanent workers in the total workforce began, falling to 62 percent in 2016.

A last but not minor detail is that the ratio of women to men has stayed relatively stable in the whole period analyzed, with a lower presence of women (6 out of every 10 workers employed are male).

Insertion Companies

Insertion companies (ICs), in a similar way to other nonprofit making entities, have become recognized in the social economy sector, as manifested by Law 5/2011, on the Social Economy, in article 5. Accordingly, their definition and characteristics place them within the sphere of initiatives based on the primacy of people and social purpose over capital, and this incorporation is visible in its recognition by different European, state level, or local public institutions (Askunze 2016).

This company type, whose object is the social-labor insertion of unemployed people in a situation of, or at risk of exclusion, existed long before the autonomous communities or the state brought them under regulation. That is why the sector demanded for years that these companies be given explicit political and legal recognition, defining and identifying the characteristics of ICs and, as well as providing legal certainty, making them subjects that receive support from the public administrations, for instance, through the development of promotion measures.

Where the legislative framework of ICs is concerned, competence in the field of labor legislation and, partially, employment policy can be said to lie exclusively with the central administration, but aspects dealing with social policies and social inclusion are the authority of the autonomous communities; this is why there is a combination, within the Spanish state, of various autonomous norms and one state law, Law 44/2017, December 13, to regulate the insertion companies system.[96]

In the case of the Autonomous Community of Euskadi, its regulations controlled ICs seven years before state law did so, with the passing of Decree 182/2008, November 11, that regulated the classification of insertion companies, and established the procedure of access to them and to their register.[97] It also legally defines this type of company in article 4.1.[98] As mentioned above, in 2007 the state passed a general law that offered a shared legislative framework for all the territories, in which a precise definition is provided, identifying a series of requirements for their constitution and functioning.

Although insertion companies do not generate the same level of employment as SECs do, their evolution over the same period was also very positive, with an increase of almost 40 percent between 2007 and 2016. The fact is that, despite various years of powerful job losses (above all in 2012 and 2014), insertion companies have managed to keep producing more jobs while taking into consideration the needs of people in situations of social exclusion or at risk of suffering from it. The main job profile continues to be insertion-related (roughly 6 out of 10), and there is a marked tendency toward convergence in gender terms where the people employed are concerned. From a situation in which women were in the majority

---

96 https://www.boe.es/buscar/act.php?id=BOE-A-2007-21492.
97 http://www.legegunea.euskadi.eus/x59-preview/es/contenidos/decreto/bopv200806515/es_def/index.shtml.
98 "1. For the purposes of the present decree, insertion companies will be deemed to be those productive structures of goods or services whose mission is the incorporation within the labor market of collectives suffering from social disadvantage or exclusion, and perform a personal project of insertion through an appropriate learning process that provides for the attainment of social and labor-related abilities, taking in basic training, labor skills, and market knowledge, which enable them to improve their conditions of employability, and meet the requirements established in the following paragraph."

Table 4.6

	Evolution of the number of Insertion Companies and of people employed in the ACE. 2000-2016									
	2007	2008	2009	2010	2011	2012	2013	2014	2015	2016
Entities	6	6	6	6	8	9	11	12	13	13
Jobs*	492	539	674	783	752	637	661	575	637	687
Women	n.a.	64,0%	62,0%	60,3%	55,9%	52,6%	49,3%	46,3%	44,6%	48,0%
Insertion	64,0%	59,9%	54,2%	59,3%	63,0%	63,0%	63,5%	61,0%	60,8%	61,6%

*Expressed in complete working days   n.a.: not available   Source: OVES/GEEB

(64 percent in 2008), there has been movement toward one of near equity between the sexes (48 percent de women in 2016), which is probably due to the inclusion in the insertion jobs of specific profiles where there is a predominance of men.

Associations and Foundations

Law 5/2011, March 29, on the Social Economy, establishes in article 5 that "associations that conduct economic activity" will be entities belonging to the sector, among others (that are already well-known), conforming to the guiding principles contained in article 4 of the Law.[99] Accordingly, our analysis will concentrate only on these modalities.

The right of association is a fundamental right provided for in the higher-ranking rules. [100] Yet its specific regulation in the Spanish state is established in Organic Law 1/2002, March 22, governing the right of association. Some autonomous communities,[101] however,

---

99 "Social economy entities act in accordance with the following guiding principles:

a) Primacy of people and social purpose over capital, involving autonomous, transparent, democratic, and participatory management conducive to the prioritization of decision-making more in terms of people and their contributions of work and services rendered to the entity, or in terms of their social purpose, than in relation with their contributions to social capital.

b) Application of the results obtained from economic activity principally in accordance with the work provided and service or activity performed by partners or by their members and, where applicable, with the social purpose pursued by the entity.

c) Promotion of solidarity, both internal and toward society, that favors a commitment to local development, equal opportunities between men and women, social cohesion, the insertion of people at risk of social exclusion, the generation of stable, quality employment, reconciliation between work, private, and family life, family and life, and sustainability.

d) Independence vis-à-vis the public authorities."
100 Article 20.1 of the Universal Declaration of Human Rights; Article 22 of the Spanish Constitution of 1978.
101 The Canary Islands, Andalusia, Euskadi, Catalonia, and the Valencian Community.

have exclusive competence in this area by virtue of their autonomy statute, and this is the case of the ACE: "By virtue of article 10.13 of the Autonomy Statute for the Basque Country this autonomous community has competence over associations that have an educational, cultural, artistic, beneficent, welfare, or similar aim, provided that they mainly carry out their operations in the Basque Country."

The Basque Parliament Law 3/1988, February 12, on Associations,[102] was the first in the state to regulate on this subject. But the passing by the state of the organic law mentioned above, in 2002, obliged the legislator to draft a new law to meet the demands of the organic legislation and to develop the contents of the previous law. The autonomous legislation currently in force is Law 7/2007, June 22, on Associations in the Basque Country,[103] which includes a clarifying definition regarding associations that is, however, in no way a closed specification.

The fundamental features that determine the latter's inclusion within the social economy are, on the one hand, the primacy of union among people, which is exactly what differentiates them from mercantile companies, and, on the other, that the economic activities they develop are exclusively aimed at achieving the purposes of the association (Díaz-Aguado 2016).

Foundations, meanwhile, have historically played a significant role in Basque social life, being conceived as nonprofit organizations whose patrimony, by the will of their founders, is employed for purposes of general interest over the long term. Today, however, foundations have extended their activities to areas of work, teaching, culture, education, research, technology, and social innovation, and new institutions have even come into being that adopt the legal status of foundations.

Basque institutions have traditionally had jurisdiction over their regulation, because it is a subject that is neither expressly provided for among the exclusive state competences in article 149 of the

---

102 https://www.boe.es/boe/dias/2012/03/13/pdfs/BOE-A-2012-3547.pdf.
103 https://www.boe.es/buscar/pdf/2011/BOE-A-2011-16287-consolidado.pdf.

Spanish Constitution,[104] nor among those assumed by the autonomous communities article 148 of the Constitution. In consequence, the Autonomous Community of Euskadi, among others, invoked article 149.3 of the Spanish Constitution, which states that matters not expressly attributed to the state may correspond to autonomous communities, by virtue of their statutes (in the case of the ACE, article 10.13 of its statute[105]).

Competence on Foundation Law in the ACE was embodied in Law 12/1994, June 17, on Foundations in the Basque Country.[106] This was recently repealed by Law 9/2016, June 2.[107] The need to adapt to the new challenges of the times and to the reality of Basque Civil Law (Law 5/2015)[108] led legislators to adopt this new legislation. On one hand, it provides greater legal certainty both to the public administration and to the foundations and civil society in general, reinforcing the right to set up such entities and establishing the controls necessary to guarantee proper compliance with the requirements of their juridical status. On the other hand, it puts in place a new sanctioning authority, so that it can act as a mechanism to discourage behaviors that run counter to administrative obligations and as a confidence-building measure for those who contribute to the financing of these types of entities.

Information on associations and foundations in the ACE is rather limited, especially where employment is concerned, as we observe in the preceding table. Nevertheless, the data available shows us that the associational fabric is genuinely broad (97 percent are associations and the remaining 3 percent corresponds to 666 foundations operational in 2016). We may add that most of the associations are of a clearly popular, transformative nature, aimed at fostering culture (58 percent of the total are engaged with "general or specific

---

104 https://www.boe.es/buscar/act.php?id=BOE-A-1978-31229.
105 "The Autonomous Community of the Basque Country has exclusive responsibility in the following areas: 13. Foundations and Associations that have an educational, cultural, artistic, beneficent, welfare or similar aim, provided that they mainly carry out their operations in the Basque Country."
106 https://www.boe.es/boe/dias/2012/02/04/pdfs/BOE-A-2012-1683.pdf
107 https://www.boe.es/buscar/doc.php?id=BOE-A-2016-6088.
108 https://www.boe.es/boe/dias/2015/07/24/pdfs/BOE-A-2015-8273.pdf.

Table 4.7

Evolution of the number of Associations and Foundations and people employed in the ACE. 2005, 2010-2016								
	2005	2010	2011	2012	2013	2014	2015	2016
Registered	14,657	20,385	21,033	21,863	21,378	21,855	22,969	23,728
People employed	6,117	12,448*	n.a.	14,075*	n.a.	n.a.	n.a.	n.a.

n.a.: not available

(*) Data referring only to Foundations and Associations of Public Interest

Source: OVES/GEEB

culture") and seeking other modes of socioeconomic relation (18 percent are of "political and socioeconomic"). The tendency for the numbers of workers almost always registered an increase in the associational and foundational fabric, above all during the first five years (between 2005 and 2010 they grew by 39 percent), while the increase after that was more moderate (at around 3 percent in annual terms). There is also a big gap between the figures presented for the number of people employed during the first five years, which is due largely to the professionalization experienced both by associations and foundations. From that point on, the number of people in work has increased, but not so brusquely.

Conclusion

Throughout the chapter we have described part of the current reality of the social economy in the ACE. As we remarked earlier, to understand the reality of the entire sector, it would be essential to consider other aspects that cannot be dealt with in a single chapter. That is why we have focused on the most representative families in the social economy.

From the outset, as in the rest of Europe, the first social economy organizations dedicated to economic activity were cooperatives and, today, they possess by far the greatest importance in socioeconomic and legal terms within the ACE, as this work has reflected. For their part, associations have were historically important and continue to be so, quantitatively and qualitatively, in generating, channeling, and strengthening different demands and struggles, aimed at covering social needs that have been "forgotten" and relegated to the future by the public authorities, or at defending collective interests, with a strong social influence. A clear example of these initiatives is provided by the different associations that have been created in society and proved crucial for the later generation of social economy experiences, as is the case of the creation of the special employment centers. It is important to highlight the work of the associations in the capitalist system, because, having no importance in monetary values when compared to other types of entities (cooperatives, worker owned companies, and so on), they have had an unquestionable and striking impact on the interests of the working class (social cohesion, the protection of nature, alternative organizational models, and suchlike).

Bearing in mind that the last period has been marked by a deep economic and social crisis of the capitalist system, and has made its inherent contradictions even more acute, the social economy has once again proved itself capable of providing a response. Our understanding is that this fortitude is not a product of chance but, on the contrary, is rooted in another way of building an economy, grounded in the people and values that characterize the social economy.

The future is far from certain, as the sociopolitical context of the coming times makes it very hard to foresee, on one hand, the attitude of the public administrations toward the sector (public policies, social clauses, recruitment, and so on), and, on the other, the direction in which the social economy is heading in the stage of growth it has embarked on.

Bibliography

Aldazabal, Javier. 2007. *Las fundaciones del sector público vasco: su régimen jurídico*. Bilbao: Lete.

Askunze, Carlos. 2016. "Empresas de inserción en la economía social. Herramientas para la inclusión sociolaboral." CIRIEC-*España: Revista jurídica de economía social y cooperativa* 29: 15–46

Agrupación de Sociedades Laborales de Euskadi. 2016. *ASLE y las sociedades laborales vascas* 1982–2016. Bilbao: ASLE.

Bengoetxea, Aitor. 2016. "Las cooperativas." CIRIEC-*España: Revista jurídica de economía social y cooperativa* 29: 205–34.

Bretos, Ignacio. 2015. "Mediación y visibilización de la economía social en el País Vasco." *Revista Vasca de Economía Social* 12: 7–34.

Díaz-Aguado, Carlos. 2016. "Empresas de inserción en la economía social. Herramientas para la inclusión sociolaboral." CIRIEC-*España: Revista jurídica de economía social y cooperativa* 29: 81–116.

Etxezarreta, Enekoitz, and Jon Morandeira. 2012. "Consideraciones conceptuales sobre la economía social a la luz de la Ley 5/2011." *Revista Vasca de Economía Social* 8: 7–36.

Fajardo, Gemma. 2008. "Aspectos societarios de la reforma de la Ley de Sociedades Laborales." CIRIEC-*España: Revista jurídica de economía social y cooperativa* 19: 141–58.

Merino, Santi. 2008. *Manual de Derecho de Sociedades Cooperativas*. *Vitoria-Gasteiz*: CSCE-EKGK; Gezki.

Moratalla, Pablo. 2015. "Los Centros Especiales de Empleo: un buen ejemplo ante la crisis económica." *In Economía Social Vasca y Crisis Económica*. Evolución entre 2009–2013, edited by Ignacio Bretos Fernández and José María Pérez de Uralde. *Donostia-San Sebastián: Observatorio Vasco de Economía Social Gizarte-Ekonomiako Euskal Behatokia*.

Observatorio Vasco de Economía Social. At www.oves-geeb.eus (last accessed October 11, 2017).

Pérez de Uralde, Jose María. 2012. "Algunas consideraciones sobre la repercusión de la Ley 5/2011, de 29 de marzo, de Economía Social en la Comunidad Autónoma de Euskadi." *Revista Vasca de Economía Social* 8: 37–61.

5

Promoting the Social Economy in the European Union and in Navarre

MIKEL IRUJO AMEZAGA

Today, the social economy is a global reality, one that has demonstrated for more than 170 years its ability to adapt to provide solutions to the needs of people around the world based on solid principles, providing an essential model for addressing the challenges our society faces. The social economy has its roots in the cooperative movement, specifically in 1844, in the English city of Rochdale. A group of workers that had lost their jobs after participating in a strike created the first cooperative store by contributing 28 shillings each, establishing the rules for the organization's operation based on the principles of cooperation and solidarity. These principles were included in the first "Cooperation Charter," which has served as the basis for the cooperative principles and the social economy for all these years (Government of Navarra, Economic Development Department 2017, 5).

The social economy employs more than eleven million workers in the European Union (EU), which is 6 percent of the total employment. This sector encompasses all entities with a specific type of legal constitution (cooperatives, foundations, associations, and mutual organizations)—many of which are also social enterprises according to the referred characteristics—and social enterprises formed either as a private company or as a conventional public limited company. The specific legal constitutions found in the social economy are especially suited to the social enterprises, since their form of governance favors participation and openness (European Commission 2011). According to statistics based on a study carried out in 2009 (Terjesen et al. 2016), the percentage of the active population dedicated to social entrepreneurship is 4.1 percent for Belgium, 7.5 percent for Finland, 3.1 percent for France, 3.3 percent for Italy, 5.4 percent for Slovenia, and 5.7 percent for the United Kingdom. Accordingly, about one in every four companies set up in Europe would be a social enterprise – a figure which rises to one in every three for Belgium, Finland, and France. These enterprises are more often found to be more productive and competitive than what is believed, due to the strong commitment on behalf of their employees and also to the fact that they offer better working conditions.

According to the European Commission, there are various challenges currently faced by the social economy, including the following:[109]

- *Difficulty to obtain access to funding*—it can be difficult for social enterprises to find the appropriate funding opportunities owing to the lack of understanding of their operational structure and their small size.

- *Low level of recognition,* making it advisable to pursue actions geared toward sharing good practices, awareness activities, and projects designed to collect statistical data of cooperatives and social enterprises.

- *Array of different legal frameworks* among the countries in the EU, and obstacles to be found in relation to the activity of some legal structures of enterprises in the social economy.

- *The lack of business skills*

---

109 http://ec.europa.eu/growth/sectors/social-economy_en.

The European Commission's Measures to Promote the Social Economy

The European Commission aims to create a level playing field in which the enterprises of the social economy can compete in an effective and fair way, without discrimination resulting from regulations and having their particular needs taken into account. To this end, the EU has approved a set of measures such as, for example, the Small Business Act;[110] the Guide to Social Innovation;[111] and the Communication on the "Social Business Initiative, which aims to build an ecosystem that promotes social enterprises in the centre of the economy and social innovation" (COM/2011/0682 final).[112] The latter includes a set of initiatives or key actions to be carried out by the EU, which has outlined a roadmap for the European Commission.

According to the cited communication, the funding system for social enterprises is underdeveloped in relation to that used by other businesses. However, there are a growing number of investors that want to combine social and environmental results with their legitimate concern of obtaining a financial return on their investment, while pursuing long-term objectives of general interest. For many social enterprises, start-up and development is wholly dependent on access to credit. However, as they are not so well known or are deemed more risky, they have more difficulty than small and medium enterprises (SMEs) in finding the necessary funding.[113]

To achieve all of this, the Commission proposes eleven key actions that fall into three different themes:

---

110 https://ec.europa.eu/growth/smes/business-friendly-environment/small-business-act_en.

111 http://publications.europa.eu/en/publication-detail/-/publication/12d044fe-617a-4131-93c2-5e0a951a095c.

112 http://eur-lex.europa.eu/legal-content/ES/TXT/HTML/?uri=CELEX:5 2011DC0682&from=EN.

113 See point 3.1 del COM/2011/0682.

1) Making it easier for social enterprises to obtain funding

Action 1: European social entrepreneurship funds.

In 2013 the Regulation (EU) No. 346/2013 came into force, on European social entrepreneurship funds, whereby a "label" was created for the European Social Entrepreneurship Funds (EuSEF), with the aim of making it easier for investors to know where their money is being invested. This label makes it easier for investors to identify and choose EuSEF; it helps social enterprises by facilitating their access to the funding and it enables investment fund managers to obtain funding with fewer complications and at reduced costs. For the marketing of investment funds that are used from this label, at least 70 percent must be invested in social enterprises. Furthermore, a fund manager must demonstrate the good conduct of the company, that it has effective systems and control measures and that it avoids any type of conflict of interest.

Action 2: Encourage the development of microcredit in Europe, by improving the related legal and institutional framework.

If it is in fact published on the website of the Commission, the link which directs you to the funding called Plan Juncker does not actually offer any specific information about social enterprises. Nevertheless, the Commission adopted the European Code of Good Conduct for Microcredit Provision, which provides recommendations and standards that should encourage the best practices within the microcredit sector. It is aimed at the microcredit providers from the point of view of the consumers, investors, donors and regulatory bodies.

Action 3: Set up an EU financial instrument to provide easier access to funding.

In 2014, the EU set up the EU Programme for Employment and Social Innovation (EaSI), a European financial instrument designed to foster a high level of sustainable and quality employment, which should contribute a reliable level of social care, tackle social exclusion and poverty, and improve working conditions. Around 21 percent of its total budget—that is, €193 million for the period 2014–2020—is earmarked for the "Microfinance and social entrepreneurship segment," following the course of the previous "Progress" program, which could grant loans of up to €25,000 for the start-up or development of an enterprise. The EaSI program does not directly fund entrepreneurs, but it allows microcredit providers in the EU to be selected in order to increase the loans by issuing collateral, and in this way share the providers' potential risk of loss.

Action 4: Make social enterprises an investment priority of the European Regional Development Fund and European Social Fund.

During the 2014–2020 programming period, the Structural Funds and the European investment funds—particularly the European Regional Development Fund (ERDF), the European Social Fund (ESF), and the Cohesion Fund—support eleven "investment priorities," also known as the thematic objectives. The Commission was able to have the social economy and social enterprises included within the Thematic Objective 9 (social inclusion, combating poverty and discrimination). This means that these themes will be able to access funding from the ERDF, ESF, and EAFRD (European Agricultural Fund for Rural Development) Funds. For example, Navarra has included it within its ESF Operational Program (Gobierno de Navarra 2015, 35).

2) Increasing the visibility of social entrepreneurship

Action 5: Identify best practices by establishing a comprehensive register of social enterprises in Europe.

In 2014 the Commission published the study *A map*

of social enterprises and their ecosystems in Europe. Having analyzed the vast diversity to be found, it revealed that only seven member states (Bulgaria, France, Italy, Luxembourg, Slovenia, Sweden, and the United Kingdom) have a framework of policies in place to encourage and support the development of social enterprises. It also presents an analysis about creating ecosystems to foster the social economy.

Action 6: Create a public database of labels and certifications applicable to social enterprises in Europe.
This action is developed in the framework of the same study mentioned under Action 5. It only presents data about the seven member states mentioned above.

Action 7: Help national and regional governments introduce measures to support, promote, and finance social enterprises.
In 2013 the Commission published the Guide to Social Innovation, which includes examples of good practices in various aspects of this policy, including a specific reference to the social economy.

Action 8: Create a multilingual information and exchange platform for social entrepreneurs, business incubators, and clusters, as well as social investors. Increase the visibility of EU programs to support social entrepreneurs and make it easier to obtain funding.
With recourse to a project funded under the framework of the Horizon 2020 program, the Commission created the Social Innovation Community. The objective is to strengthen, connect, and enable existing communities of social innovation to grow, including the innovation of the public sector, digital social innovation, intermediaries and agents of the social economy, and others. It includes the setting up of a social economy network.
3) Improving the legal environment

Action 9: Simplify the rules regarding legal recognition as a European Cooperative Society; put forward a regulation creating a legal status for European foundations.
In 2003, the Statute for a European Cooperative was adopted. The truth of this matter is that since 2012—when the Proposal for a Council Regulation on the Statute for a European Foundation (2012) was introduced—there have not been any further developments.

Action 10: Make quality and working conditions more important criteria for the awarding of public procurement contracts, particularly for social and health services.
Through the directives on public procurement contracts of 2014, a set of social criteria aimed at promoting the social economy was introduced by means of this policy. It introduced more flexible standards and, above all, elements that had not existed previously such as, for example, social innovation (European Commission 2014).

Action 11: Simplify the rules for awarding public aid to social and local services (which would benefit many social enterprises).
The Commission publishes different reports and studies on the simplification of the process of applying standards relating to public aid received by social and local services.

Other Measures to Promote the Social Economy

As in the case of other cross-disciplinary policies, there are opportunities to fund social economy projects through various instruments, such as H2020, COSME (Competitiveness for Enterprises and Small and Medium-sized Enterprises), Erasmus+, as well as EaSI and other Structural Funds already mentioned in the previous section.

The largest innovation instrument—the Horizon 2020[114] program—includes a line about Collective Awareness Platforms for
Sustainability and Social Innovation (CAPS), which covers the following four priority areas: Collective awareness pilots for bottom-up
participation in innovation paradigms (R&I [Research and Innovation]
small actions – €24 million); Multidisciplinary research on collective
awareness platforms (Internet Science) (R&I small actions – €4 million); Digital Social Platforms (R&I small actions – €7 million); and
coordinating activities in CAPS (CSAs [Coordination and Support
Actions] – €1 million).

Alternatively, there is the SME Instrument, which is a sub-program
of the eighth European Marco-Financial Assistance Programme of
the Horizon 2020 R&D&I (Research, Development, and Innovation), and whose focus is exclusively aimed at small and medium-
sized enterprises. Funding from this sub-program will be applied
to all types of innovation, including nontechnological innovations
and those relating to services. The projects presented within this
program can be individual or group projects, set up by SMEs, and
they receive funding throughout the whole of the innovation process by means of a scheme of providing subsidies in phases. This is
aimed at providing support to those traditional SMEs or innovators
who have ambitions to grow and to develop and internationalize
their business activities through a European innovation project.[115]

It is also possible to find examples of social economy projects
funded under the umbrella of Erasmus+.[116]

At the same time, the Commission organizes various awards, to
which those engaged in social innovation can apply.

---

114 https://ec.europa.eu/digital-single-market/en/collective-awareness.
115 http://www.horizon2020.es/instrumento-pyme/.
116 For example, Erasmus+ SIRCle (http://www.sircle-project.eu/): The Social
    Innovation for Resilient Communities (SIRCle) project uses adult education
    and a training curriculum known as "The Evoneers' Journey" to address one
    of the most pressing needs of our time, namely to combine our commitment
    to the wellbeing of the planet and to a more sustainable society with our
    ability to be financially sustainable.

- European Social Innovation Competition:[117] The objective is to foster inclusive growth by means of promoting ideas generated by people who have the necessary skills to be competitive in a changing economy. Innovators who create business models that promote equality of opportunities facilitating access to new technologies can apply. The award is open to entrepreneurs, social innovators, students, designers, makers, technology enthusiasts, educators, and people of diverse backgrounds from across Europe.

- Horizon 2020 Award for Social Innovation (2015).[118]

- RegioStars Award,[119] which identifies good practices in regional development and highlights original and innovative projects that are attractive and inspiring for other regions.

- Social Innovation Tournament,[120] which recognizes and supports the best European social entrepreneurs. It is organized annually in a different country to reward and endorse European entrepreneurs whose main objective is to generate social, ethical, or environmental impact. Endowed with between €20,000 and €50,000, the projects are usually concerned with combating unemployment, the marginalization of underprivileged communities, and the promotion of access to education in a wide range of fields, from teaching and healthcare to the natural or urban environment, using new technologies, new systems, and new processes.

---

117 https://ec.europa.eu/growth/industry/innovation/policy/social/competition_en.

118 http://ec.europa.eu/research/horizonprize/index.cfm?prize=social-innovation.

119 http://ec.europa.eu/regional_policy/en/regio-stars-awards.

120 https://institute.eib.org/social-innovation-tournament-2.

The following is a list of all projects funded by the EU within the scope of the social economy: BENISI (Building a European Network of Incubators for Social Innovation); CRESSI (Creating Economic Space for Social Innovation); EFESEIIS (Enabling the Flourishing and Evolution of Social Entrepreneurship for Innovative and Inclusive Societies); ITSSOIN (Impact of the Third Sector as Social Innovation); SEFORIS (Social Enterprise as Force for More Inclusive and Innovative Societies); SI-DRIVE (Social Innovation: Driving Force of Social Change); SIMPACT (Boosting the Impact of Social Innovation in Europe through Economic Underpinnings); Third Sector Impact – The Contribution of the Third Sector to Europe's Socio-economic Development; and TRANSITION (Trans-national Network for Social Innovation Incubation).

Social Economy Networks and Initiatives in the EU

There are several networks and initiatives of a private scope relating to the social economy that primarily aim to influence the European institutions. It is always interesting to know about their activities, since these networks normally consist of the groups and entities of the social economy from different member states, and their activity is of fundamental importance to the task of monitoring the current state of these affairs in Brussels. The most important ones are: Social Economy Europe; ENSIE (European Network of Social Integration Enterprises); CECOP – CICOPA Europe (Con-fédération européenne des coopératives de production – Comité International des Coopératives de Production et Artisanales), the European Confederation of Industrial and Service Cooperatives; Cooperatives Europe; GECES (Groupe d'experts de la Commission sur l'entrepreneuriat social, European Commission Experts Group on Social Entrepreneurship); REVES (Réseau Européen des Villes et Régions de l'Économie Sociale, European Network of Cities and Regions for Social Economy); Social Services Europe; ERRIN (European Regions and Research Innovation Network), the best regional network on a practical level. This is a very good platform to organize an event in Brussels with invitation to other regions; and the European Parliament's Social Economy Intergroup.

The networks usually comprise members from the member states. On the one hand, they may be networks of associations from the social economy sphere, such as the cited *Social Economy Europe*, consisting of state associations of bodies promoting the social economy. On the other hand, they may be networks composed of entities or companies from the private domain, such as the cited *Cooperatives Europe*. They can also be networks or associations of a political nature, such as the European Parliament's Social Economy Intergroup, composed entirely of the chamber's MEPs (Members of the European Parliament) and which is clearly focused on lobbying and influencing the Commission and the Council of the European Union.

Outlook and Future of the Social Economy in the EU

Development of the social economy is officially one of the top priorities of the EU. However, there is still a lack of direct support mechanisms, as well as the need for a better legislative ecosystem that supports this development. According to a study by Quentin Liger, Marco Stefan, and Jess Britton (2016, 77):

> Despite changes in policies with respect to social enterprises, at the regional, national and European levels, a restricted view on the social economy coupled with a silo–approach in the development of supportive policy measures still hinders the development of the field, as well as its measurement, assessment and recognition. The possibility for social economy actors to access and operate within the Single Market and to contribute on their part to European economic growth depends to a great extent on the elimination of comparative disadvantages currently hindering their capacity to compete with other traditional economic actors in the production of goods and services. The analysis conducted in the

framework of this study has allowed the identification of a series of structural, regulatory and financial barriers, which still affect this segment of the economy.

This study underlined the fact that, "there is a need to harmonise different European legal environments for social economy enterprises, allowing social economy enterprises and organizations (particularly mutuals, associations, foundations and work integration social enterprises) to operate (cross-border) in the internal market, on an equal footing with other forms of enterprises" (ibid.). It also underlined the fact that difficulties in accessing adequate financial instruments affect most social economy actors and their capacity to develop entrepreneurial activities in Europe. Finally, it was very critical about the "lack of visibility and understanding of the social economy enterprise model. For instance, it will be important for EU institutions to intervene, so that all Member States include social economy enterprises in their business education as part of the national curriculum, for all education levels" (ibid.).

That apart, the already mentioned European Commission Experts Group on Social Entrepreneurship (GECES) called for action on the part of the European Commission, EU countries, and social enterprises organizations (Expert Group on Social Entrepreneurship (GECES) 2016). It argued for a European Action Plan for the Social Economy and Social Enterprises that would provide new impetus to promote an enabling environment for social enterprises and the social economy to flourish, building on their core values such as democratic governance, social impact, innovation, profit reinvestment, and the central place given to the human in the economy. The report suggests a series of key recommendations for policymakers to support the development of social enterprises and the social economy as a driving force of inclusive and impactful economic growth and it is cs structured according to four key thematic areas, such as increasing visibility and understanding of social enterprises, helping social enterprises to access finance, improving the legal environment, and driving economic growth.

Among the thirteen recommendations, it highlights the need to support a stronger place for social enterprise in public policy and actions at all levels, and for the Commission, EU countries, and their local and regional authorities to mainstream the social economy and social enterprises in all significant policies, programs, and practices. This would involve including social enterprises as eligible entities in all relevant European funding programs, promoting the participation of the social economy and social enterprises in important European mobility schemes, and promoting mutual learning and capacity building between regional and local authorities so as to develop integrated support strategies.

The report also calls for a development of a European economic environment that enables the social economy and social enterprises to access finance. Recommendations in this area address the capacity building, financing, and infrastructure needs of social enterprises. Specifically, it is recommended that increased resources be provided to training programs, incubators and intermediaries that provide tailored capacity building support, and helping social enterprises to build their managerial skills and achieve financial sustainability. Concrete measures to unlock more funding that is better suited to social enterprises include awareness building among the broader funding community about how to finance social enterprises, building capacity within the "impact community," enhancing the suitability of social investment, alleviating regulatory hurdles and the mapping of existing tax incentives associated with investment in social enterprise in order to disseminate best practice. Public funding should continue to be directed to social enterprises and also be used to mobilize private capital, through investment in and de-risking of social enterprise funding, as well as by putting proper governance structures in place.

Improving the legal environment is also both a challenge and a need. The report also calls for facilitating the development of an ecosystem within which social enterprises can thrive, and a number of key recommendations have been made with respect to the legal environment and the provision of legal and regulatory frameworks to encourage the creation and development of the social economy and social enterprises. The final section in the report deals with measures to help the social economy and social enterprises reach their potential as key drivers of equitable and socially-inclusive economic growth. The aim here is to increase EU support for social enterprises within the context of international development, with a view to achieving the post-2015 Sustainable Development Goals.

The Commission was already asked about these recommendations during the Plenary of the European Parliament that was held in October 2017. Věra Jourová, European Commissioner for Justice, Consumers, and Gender Equality, stressed that, "we want to see the social economy succeed as it offers innovative answers to societal challenges, and replies to the growing demand of citizens and consumers for a new way of doing business responsibly and sustainably." Jourová recognized that, "there is untapped potential and barriers which hamper the development of the sector in many countries." Therefore, she explained that in 2017 the Commission decided—under the start-up and scale-up Initiative—to launch new concrete actions to stimulate the development of the social economy. Commissioner Jourová announced that good progress has been made but there are still a number of measures that need to be implemented in 2018. In this regard, she stressed that launching a European Action Plan for the Social Economy would be premature: "we want to deliver what we have promised and, then, let us see if more needs to be done." To conclude, Commissioner Jourová stressed that, "we will continue to work with all stakeholders to ensure that the voice of the social economy is heard across the whole Europe."[121]

---

121 http://www.socialeconomy.eu.org/blog/european-parliament-debates-european-action-plan-social-economy.

Navarre and the Social Economy

In 2016, Navarre updated its Smart Specialization Strategies (henceforth, S3). The S3 is a model for the economic development that involves concentrating the resources of the economic areas in which each region has significant competitive advantages. To this end, the S3 requires the development of a shared vision of the future and the identification—through a process called "entrepreneurial discovery"—of thematic priorities, bearing in mind the economic, scientific, and technological potential and the global competitiveness of the region and its players, especially enterprises. Finally, the S3 proposes the use of smart policies focused on these priorities in order to maximize the potential of regional development, and in this way move toward a knowledge-based economy.

Navarre's S3 includes an assessment, a strategic vision of Navarre 2030, and it establishes a set of thematic priorities that are divided into economic areas (such as automation, food chain, healthcare. and renewable energies) and factors of competitiveness. One of these factors of competitiveness is business development. Navarre's strategy states that it must

> Facilitate the transformation of Navarra's industrial fabric in order to guide it into the industry of the future: more competitive, more technological, more innovative, more sustainable and more committed to society and the environment. Strengthen the business competitiveness through the cluster model and policies of growth and internationalization. Build a new business model through organisational innovation and participation of the workforce, thereby consolidating a working climate of trust[122].

The S3 also identifies the main tools required to develop this objective, such as the preparation of an industrial plan, a clusters policy, an entrepreneurship plan, an internationalization plan and, why not, the preparation of a Social Economy Plan. At the same

---

122 Navarra's Smart Specialization Strategy; http://www.sodena.com/index.php/en/estrategia-regional.html

time, Navarre's S3 includes the approval of the Social Economy Plan as one of the instruments to be used for its implementation.

There are other references to sectors of the social economy such as, for example, when the food chain industry is selected as one of the key sectors, it is partly due to "the existence of a rich fabric of co-operatives and independent entrepreneurs."

As stated, the S3 should serve to develop the potential strengths of Navarre, since it serves as a guide for the government to implement its policies. For this reason, in reference to the mandate set out in the S3, during 2017 the government of Navarre approved the Comprehensive Social Economy Plan of Navarre for the period 2017–2020.

Navarre is one of the autonomous communities in which the social economy has great importance and deep roots, as is evident from sector data and the SWOT analysis prepared for defining the strategy of the plan:

- For its contribution to employment, which was especially important during the long and hard period of crisis, exceeding the number of existing jobs before the crisis in the sector, responding to companies in crisis to continue activity and employment, and ranking third among the autonomous communities in the percentage of social economy employment.

- For its qualitative and differential contribution to employment, a different, participatory, and responsible employment model; more stable and sustainable employment; more solidarity and more inclusion; employment linked to the region and its resources; an employment of the people and not human resources; collective employment and not employment numbers.

  - For its connection to the region of social economy companies, they are companies that are not relocated, and agro-food cooperatives are implanted throughout the region. All contribute to the regional structure, the generation and maintenance of the business activity, and employment within the territory.

- For the number of people working in foundations and associations supporting the activity of public institutions; because of the results of job insertion of people in a situation and at risk of exclusion; because of the involvement in the solidarity economy.

- For its contribution to entrepreneurship, a model of collective entrepreneurship with people from the region and located in the region, and a basis for the future business fabric, working with the pool of professionals. Thus, social economy companies created in 2015 exceeded 7 percent of the total of companies created in Navarre, twice as much as before the crisis.

- For the strong roots of social economy businesses, with a presence in all business sectors, ranking third among autonomous communities in relative employment number; with social economy companies innovating, exporting and creating jobs; and with businesses and business groups serving as a model of reference.

Navarre's social economy sector also includes special employment non-profit centers that do not have an organization that represents them, as well as associations that carry out socially based economic activities in Navarre. The lack of regular and complete statistics about the social economy sector remains an obstacle for a proper diagnosis of the sector as a whole. However, on the basis of the existing data, the figures for Navarre's social economy for 2015, corresponding to the families previously described, are as follows: •1,064 social economy businesses; 16,430 employed people, representing more than 7 percent of the working population in the private sector in Navarre; a €1.953 billion estimated turnover; and more than 28,000 associates and volunteers in social economy companies.

The majority of companies and employment—more than 60 percent—is concentrated around cooperatives and labor companies, mainly associated work companies, although there is also a substantial number of entities and employment in foundations – more than 20 percent. The largest part of the turnover is concentrated again in cooperatives and labor companies (more than 95 percent), although here the largest contribution corresponds to agro-food cooperatives. The same occurs with the number of members.

With regard to the evolution of these figures during these years, it should be noted that, in 2015, the number of employed people reached the same level that it had been before the crisis and the turnover of the entire social economy sector continued to increase during these years.

The analysis prepared for the Comprehensive Social Economy Plan (Government of Navarra, Economic Development Department 2017, 5) identifies important and specific opportunities for Navarre's social economy. It concludes that there is potential for the development and growth of the social economy and its role in Navarre's socioeconomic development, fundamentally its contribution to employment and social transformation. In order to enhance the results of the social economy, a comprehensive strategic social economy plan has been put forward: vertical integration through a set of complementary actions, temporary integration combining short-term and long-term actions, and horizontal integration including actions by the different social economy families, seeking synergies and complementarities among them.

At the same time, this plan seeks to align all companies, organizations, and agents of the social economy in a common strategy, in collaboration with the administration; that is, as participants of the same project, from the design phase onward, in order to work in coordination toward the same goal. In order to make the most of this potential, public policy support of the development of the actions envisaged by the Comprehensive Social Economy Plan is not sufficient on its own. It is also necessary to integrate the social economy into all of Navarre's policies on a cross-cutting basis.

Conclusion

The social economy continues to be a great unknown in various member states of the EU, even in large sectors of many of those states or sub-state regions—such as Navarre—in which it has been strongly embedded. Nevertheless, it is proving to be an extremely resilient sector for withstanding hard-hitting economic crises. The years of the most severe economic recession (2008–2013) were accompanied by a dramatic increase in unemployment (in Navarre it reached 15 percent of the active population, which is double the rate it had prior to the crisis). In this context, the number of active jobs held in enterprises of the social economy in Navarre actually increased, which is evidence of the strength of this sector in reinforcing both the quality and the stability of employment.

On the other hand, the social economy brings with it an increased stability in the business environment and attracts more investment to the region. It should be noted that the importance of industry in Navarre is considerable – reaching almost 30 percent of the total economic activity, while the EU average is 16 percent. Even so, Navarre is too exposed to corporate capital from outside of the region, and this means that the decision-making level of many of the large industries is usually concentrated in Madrid or in other capital cities of EU countries. Nevertheless, enterprises of the social economy tend to be more deeply rooted in the territory than in other sectors of the economy. The aforementioned Smart Specialization Strategy of Navarre specifically refers to a cooperative movement, an example of which is the AN Group: a cooperative that is more than one hundred years old and dedicated to the agrofood industry but that has also diversified into areas of the energy and insurance sectors, with an annual turnover that comes close to one billion dollars. Also worth noting is the Mondragon Group, a global industrial cooperative that contributes almost 1.3 percent of Navarre's GDP with more than four thousand direct jobs – second only to the Volkswagen Group.

Thus, the deep-rootedness and strong connection with the region is one of the key factors of the social economy. In addition to this, there is a model of governance that gives more importance to well-being and job stability over capital. The worker is the protagonist of the social economy. Direct participation in the decision making means that this is a unique type of governance and is incomparable to other sectors. Investments are made with consideration given to both the workers and to the social dimension and impact they may have on the region, while at the same time never losing sight of the competitiveness of companies, as they have to continue operating in a changing and demanding international environment.

All these factors lead one to reflect on the very existence of the European Union. The first articles of the Treaty on European Union provide an overview of the values on which it was founded. These are: respect for human dignity, freedom, and equality. It also highlights the values shared by the member states, such as pluralism, non-discrimination, tolerance, justice, solidarity, and equality between men and women, among other things. The treaty also states that decisions must be taken as openly and as close to the citizens as possible. In addition to all of this there is Article 50, according to which, every member state will be able to decide, in accordance with its constitutional laws, to withdraw from the EU. In other words, membership is voluntary.

All of the points covered here present a striking similarity between the values upheld by the EU and those on which the social economy is based. The test for the social economy—one that has already been surpassed—is to demonstrate that profitability, competitiveness, and the development of the business sector are not in polar opposition to developing a greater well-being and dignity of the workers and of society overall. I would go as far as to say that the social economy is at the very heart of the values on which the European Union is based, and it is for this very reason that I believe that a demand for a more extensive development of this policy ought to be placed among the top priorities of all the European institutions.

Bibliography

European Commission. 2011. *Social Business Initiative: Creating a Favourable Climate for Social Enterprises, Key Stakeholders in the Social Economy and Innovation.* Brussels: European Commission. At https://eur-lex.europa.eu/legal-content/EN/TXT/HTML/?uri=CELEX:52011DC0682&from= EN.

————. 2012. The New State Aid Rules for Services of General Economic Interest. At http://ec.europa.eu/competition/publications/cpn/2012_1_9_en.pdf.

————. 2014. Procurement Opportunities for Social Enterprises Under the new EU procurement rules. Brussels: European Commission. At http://ec.europa.eu/DocsRoom/documents/12965/attachments/6/translations. Expert Group on Social Entrepreneurship (GECES). 2016. Social Enterprises and the Social Economy Going Forward. Brussels: European Commission. At http://ec.europa.eu/growth/content/social-enterprises-and-social-economy-going-forward-0_en.

Gobierno de Navarra. 2015. Programa Operativo FSE de Navarra 2014–2020. N.p: N.p. At http://repositori.uji.es/xmlui/bitstream/handle/10234/167831/P.O._FSE_14-20_NAVARRA.pdf?sequence=1.

Government of Navarra, Economic Development Department. 2017. Comprehensive Social Economy Plan of Navarra 2017–2020. N.p: Government of Navarra. At http://na.bruselas.site/es/comprehensive-social-economy-plan-navarra-2017-2020.

Liger, Quentin, Marco Stefan, and Jess Britton. 2016. Social Economy. Brussels: Directorate General for Internal Policies. European Parliament, IP/A/IMCO/2015-08. At http://www.europarl.europa.eu/RegData/etudes/STUD/2016/578969/IPOL_STU(2016)578969_EN.pdf.

Terjesen, Siri, Jan Lepoutre, Rachida Justo, and Niels Bosma. 2016. Global Entrepreneurship Monitor Report on Social Entrepreneurship. London: Global Entrepreneurship Research Association.

Websites

http://www.socialeconomy.eu.org/blog/european-parliament-debates-european-action-plan-social-economy.

http://www.gemconsortium.org/about.aspx?page=pub_gem_special_topic_reports.

http://ec.europa.eu/growth/sectors/social-economy_en.

https://ec.europa.eu/growth/smes/business-friendly-environment/small-business-act_en. http://publications.europa.eu/en/publication-detail/-/publication/12d044fe-617a-4131-93c2-5e0a951a095c.

http://eur-lex.europa.eu/legal-content/ES/TXT/HTML/?uri=CELEX:52011DC0682&from=EN.

https://ec.europa.eu/info/law/european-social-entrepreneurship-funds-eusef-regulation-eu-no-346-2013_en.

https://ec.europa.eu/commission/commissioners/2014-2019/katainen/announcements/juncker-plan-supports-400-microbusinesses-luxembourg_en.

http://ec.europa.eu/growth/tools-databases/newsroom/cf/itemdetail.cfm?item_id=5479&lang=en.

http://ec.europa.eu/social/main.jsp?catId=836&langId=en.

http://ec.europa.eu/regional_policy/sources/docgener/informat/2014/guidance_social_economy.pdf.

http://repositori.uji.es/xmlui/bitstream/handle/10234/167831/P.O._FSE_14-20_NAVARRA.pdf?sequence=1.

http://ec.europa.eu/social/main.jsp?langId=en&catId=89&newsId=2149&furtherNews=yes.

http://s3platform.jrc.ec.europa.eu/documents/20182/84453/Guide_to_Social_Innovation.pdf.

https://ec.europa.eu/growth/single-market/public-procurement/rules-implementation_en. http://ec.europa.eu/DocsRoom/documents/12965/attachments/6/translations.

http://ec.europa.eu/competition/publications/cpn/2012_1_9_en.pdf.

http://ec.europa.eu/competition/state_aid/overview/new_guide_eu_
rules_procurement_en.pdf.

http://ec.europa.eu/DocsRoom/documents/14608/attachments/48/
translations.

https://ec.europa.eu/digital-single-market/en/collective-awareness.

http://www.horizon2020.es/instrumento-pyme/.

https://ec.europa.eu/growth/industry/innovation/policy/social/com-
petition_en.

http://ec.europa.eu/research/horizonprize/index.cfm?prize=social-
innovation.

http://ec.europa.eu/regional_policy/en/regio-stars-awards.

https://institute.eib.org/social-innovation-tournament-2.

6

Theoretical Approach to the Typology of Public Policies for the Advancement of the Social Economy in Europe[123]

JON MORANDEIRA ARCA AND ANE ETXEBARRIA RUBIO

The objective of this work is to analyze the theoretical framework of public policies in Europe addressed to foster, disseminate, and develop the social economy. In this regard, the study of social economy public policies should be focused on differentiating between policies that affect the structure of the sector, supporting the

123 This work is part of a research project by Jon Morandeira (2013) that was used as the foundation for the roundtable "Public Policies for the Promotion of the Social Economy: Reality, Challenges, and Opportunities" during the social economy conference "The Reality of the Social Economy in the Euro-region: A Cross-border Perspective," organized by GEZKI, attached to the UPV/EHU, in collaboration with the Basque government, the Government of Navarre, and the Center for Basque Studies at the University of Nevada, Reno. Activity conducted within the framework of the Research Group "Gizarte Ekonomia eta bere Zuzenbidea," GIU17/052, attached to the GEZKI Institute, University of the Basque Country (UPV/EHU).

creation and development of entities, and employment policies that directly affect employment in them.

Accordingly, the present work comprises five headings. Following this brief introduction, the second heading analyzes and synthesizes the theoretical framework for the typology of social economy public policies. The third section expands on the policies aimed at social economy entities, while the fourth, following the outline laid out under the second heading, deals with policies aimed at employment in the social economy entities themselves. Last, the study ends with a section devoted to final considerations concerning the analysis conducted.

Typologies of Social Economy Public Policies in Europe

The articulation of public policies supporting the social economy by policymakers and social agents depends on the degree to which they are aware of recognizing the sector's capacity to remedy social and economic imbalances, contributing to the achievement of different objectives of general interest that encourage endogenous economic development, correct deficits in social services, contribute to social cohesion and the distribution of wealth, and address imbalances in the job market (Chaves and Monzón 2000). For it is in the social economy where the greatest added social value is produced, in the areas of employment, social cohesion, the generation of social and economic fabric, the development of democracy, social innovation, and local development (Chaves 2012, 175).

But there are two more arguments that justify public intervention in the social economy (Chaves 2010, 572 and 2012, 174), in addition to the satisfaction of social needs. On the one hand, governments must ensure conditions of economic pluralism, guaranteeing the equal opportunity of all economic agents. And, on the other, different market failures[124] must be corrected, along with "institutional

---

124 Information asymmetries, financing asymmetries, problems associated with human capital training, resource assignment problems in technological and

failures" because of their particular institutional nature based on democracy and the specific distribution of surpluses and profits.

The study of social economy public policies must involve a focus that distinguishes between social economy public policies that affect the sector's structure, supporting the creation and development of entities, and employment policies that directly impact on employment in social economy entities (Chaves and Monzón 2000 and Chaves 2008).

Table 6.1: Social Economy public policies

POLICIES aimed at Social Economy entities
 	
  - Supply policies (vis-à-vis the organizations' structure)
 	
    - Institutional measures
 	
    - Financial measures
 	
    - Measures of economic support with real services
 	
  - Demand policies (vis-à-vis the organizations' activity)

POLICIES aimed at employment in Social Economy entities
 	
  - Support measures for the creation and stabilization of employment in the Social Economy
 	
  - Support measures for training in the Social Economy
 	
  - Other measures

Source: Chaves (2008).

Another classification of public policies aimed at the social economy based on the nature of the instruments or measures utilized was made by Jose Luis Monzón, Rafael Calvo, Rafael Chaves, Isabel Gemma Fajardo, and Fernando Valdés (2009, 92) (See Table 2).

---

organizational innovation processes, and problems of access to public and international markets (Fonfría 2006).

Table 6.2:
Categorization of policies aimed at the Social Economy

Institutional measures	1. Recognition of the Social Economy as a Private Actor. 2. Recognition of the operational capacity of the Social Economy in all sectors of economic activity. 3. Recognition of the Social Economy as a Political Actor. 4. Recognition of the Social Economy as an Actor that is an Executor of policies. 5. Public bodies promoting the Social Economy.
Cognitive Measures	6. Dissemination and knowledge of the Social Economy throughout society. 7. Social Economy Training. 8. Social Economy Research.
Economic Measures	9. Budgetary measures. 10. Fiscal measures. 11. Other financial support measures. 12. Technical support measures.

Source: Monzón, et al. (2009: 92).

Yet, since the main instruments of public intervention in the private sector are public coercion, information, and incentives, Chaves (2010 and 2012) categorizes social economy promotion policies within two large groups: soft policies and hard policies (Table 3). The former are aimed at establishing an appropriate environment or institutional and cultural environmental framework in which they can emerge, operate, and be developed; the second set of policies is directed at the entities themselves as economic/business units.

Table 6.3:
Typologies of policies aimed at the Social Economy

Soft policies. Policies aimed at creating a favorable environment
Institutional measures
• Aimed at the legal structure as a Private Actor. • Recognizing the operational capacity of the Social Economy in all sectors of economic activity. • Recognizing the Social Economy as a Political Actor, an interlocutor in the development and execution of public policies. • Driving public bodies that promote the Social Economy.
Measures of a cognitive nature
• For dissemination and knowledge of the Social Economy in society. • For the promotion of training in the Social Economy area. • For the promotion of Social Economy research.
Hard policies. Economic Policies for business promotion
Supply measures: **Measures aimed at improving competitiveness**
• Budgetary, fiscal, and financial support measures; technical, training, and similar support measures. They are characterized by their approach to the company life cycle (whether the firm is at the set-up stage or undergoing its business development) and the business function that requires reinforcement (financing, consultancy/advisory services, training, employment and human resource management, cooperation and networks, R+D and innovation, quality, new information and communication technologies, physical space, etc.).
Demand measures: Measures aimed at level of activity
• Facilitating access to foreign markets and public markets.

Source: Jon Morandeira (2013: 184).

These classifications differ not only in the contents but in the actual ranking, which is why the following classification is proposed, based on those made by Chaves (2002, 457; 2008, 41; 2010, 573; and 2012, 177) and Monzón et al. (2009, 92) (See Table 4).

Table 6.4:
Social Economy Public Policies

POLICIES aimed at Social Economy entities		
Supply policies (vis-à-vis the organizations' structure)		
Institutional measures	• Recognition of the Social Economy as a Private Actor. • Recognition of the operational capacity of the Social Economy in all sectors of economic activity. • Recognition of the Social Economy as a Political Actor. • Public bodies promoting the Social Economy	*Soft policies*
Cognitive Measures	• Dissemination, training, and Social Economy research.	*Soft policies*
Economic Measures	• Budgetary measures. • Fiscal measures. • Other financial support measures. • Technical support measures.	*Hard policies*
Demand policies (vis-à-vis the organizations' activity)		
• Measures of access to the status of supplier to the Public Administration. • Measures of regulation and application of public-private partnerships with the Social Economy.		*Hard policies*
POLICIES aimed at employment in Social Economy entities		
• Support measures for the creation and stabilization of employment in the Social Economy. • Support measures for Social Economy training. • Other measures.		*Hard policies*

Source: Morandeira (2013: 185).

Public Policies Aimed at Social Economy Entities

In accordance with the outline proposed in the foregoing section (See Table 4), and with Chaves (2002, 2008, and 2012), Monzón et al. (2009), and Baleren Bakaikoa and Jon Morandeira (2012) as guidelines, we now delimit and describe the different measures that comprise social economy public policies.

Supply Policies

As indicated in Table 4, supply policies are aimed at the structure of social economy entities. First, institutional and cognitive measures whose purpose is to provide the social economy with a systemic space can be distinguished, and, in second place, there are economic measures designed to improve the efficiency and effectiveness of social economy entities.

Institutional Measures

The institutional framework that governs the social economy lends it a systemic space, recognizing it as an economic and social actor in the process of development and application of public policies (Chaves 2008 and Monzón et al. 2009). As the table above indicates, the following functions can be identified:

- Recognition of the social economy as a private actor: These measures refer to legal and statutory aspects of social economy entities. In the dynamic setting we inhabit, legislation must be adapted to the new demands of this environment, encouraging the social economy, as its development might otherwise be limited. "The adaptation of the legal regulations to the new demands of agents favors their recognition, emergence, and development" (Monzón et al. 2009, 93).

- Recognition of the operational capacity of the social economy in all sectors of economic activity: Legislation can raise important barriers to access and to the free development of some activities conducted by social economy entities.

It seems reasonable, given the similar nature of the above two measures, to consider them as the same measure within the institutional measures (Bakaikoa and Morandeira 2012, 238).

Recognition of the Social Economy as a Political Actor

This concerns the existence of institutionalized bodies for participation and social dialogue with representation from the social economy, taking part in public policy development processes. Following Yves Vaillancourt (2009), four kinds of scenarios can be differentiated in terms of the way in which external actors are integrated (Chaves 2012 and Teresa Savall 2013):

- Mono-construction: the state takes unilateral decisions about the development of public policies, without consultation with external agents. This model is the opposite of the idea of co-construction.

- Neoliberal co-construction: the state includes social groups in the private sector that possess greater socioeconomic power. This model only benefits the social groups that participate in the process, excluding the goal of general interest.

- Corporativist co-construction: the state offers the opportunity for social agents to take part, but only groups that have a greater capacity of organization to exert pressure in decision-making participate in dialogue for the development of policies.

- Co-construction based on democracy and solidarity: the state, although it will have the last word, can rely on participation both from market agents and from civil society in the policy development process.

- Public bodies for the promotion of the social economy. These are bodies within the public administration with responsibilities for the social economy, established as an indicator of the degree of recognition and prioritization of policymakers, and acting as a powerful driving force for visibility and a sociopolitical image, in addition to other effects upon the political process including information and coordination.

Cognitive Measures

Dissemination, training, and research policies are designed to furnish visibility and social receptivity, and to develop competences in training and research.

Specifically, these are measures in favor of the presence of the social economy in the study plans of educational establishments at the high school, professional, and university level, in public employment services, and private professional services for the counseling and creation of firms, and in support of the existence of public, public-private, or specific private centers.

Economic Measures

- Budgetary measures. These are budgeary items and/or programs aimed at promoing the structure of social economy entities, operationalized in the form of subsidies.

- Fiscal measures. In this case, this is a spcific fiscal tax system to facilitate the consolidationand development of the social economy.

- Other financial support measures. Measures aimed at enabling social economy entities to acess credit. Here we distinguish between legislative measures[125] and public participation in financial bodies in support of the social economy.

---

125 These legislative measures are closely related to recognition of the social economy as a private actor but, given their economic nature, it seems more appropriate to keep them in a separate category.

- Technical support measures. These are also designated as technical support measures backed up by real services. Public structures for developing the social economy through the provision of technical services of information, training, research, advice, and so on. These structures can be provided in three modalities and may be managed in a centralized or decentralized fashion within the public administration:

  - Passive structures: they are confined to supporting social economy initiatives.

  - Catalyzing structures: they directly stimulate the creation of development initiatives within the social economy.

  - Proactive structures: they carry out public initiatives for the development of the social economy.

Demand Policies

Demand policies seek to impact on the activity level of social economy entities, building on the principle that a selective increase in public spending generates an increase in their activity level. Their aim is, therefore, to facilitate the social economy's access to the status of supplier of goods and services to the public sector.

Measures of Access to the Status of Supplier to the Public Administration: Social Clauses

Access to the status of supplier to the public administration occurs through what are known as social clauses in the public administrations' procurements (Lesmes 2008), accepted at a European level following the adoption of Directive 2004/18/EC by the European Parliament and the European Council concerning coordination of procurement procedures for public works contracts, public supply contracts, and public service contracts: "A contracting authority may use criteria aimed at meeting social requirements, in response in particular to the needs—defined in the specifications of the contract—of particularly disadvantaged groups of people."

These mechanisms are gathered under the concept of social purchase that "considers aspects such as employment quality, gender perspective, the hiring of disabled people or the hiring of insertion companies and special employment centers, support for the social economy and small and medium enterprises, the promotion of equal opportunities and universal accessibility and design, and the promotion of corporate social responsibility," which, along with green purchase and ethical purchase, shapes the conception of sustainable public purchase (Lesmes and Rodríguez 2010, 10).

Under Directive 2004/18/EC, Lesmes and Rodríguez (2010, 43–66) specify the seven stages of the procurement process adapted for the incorporation of social criteria:

1. Determination of the subject of contract: the contracting authority is free to define the subject of contract that best fits its needs, with the right to incorporate social considerations,[126] respecting the principles of nondiscrimination and free circulation of goods and services.

2. Technical specifications: in an objective and detailed manner the characteristics required of the tenderers are fixed so that the product, job, or service meets the stated aims.

3. Reserved contracts: contracts are reserved for entities of a social nature (principally special employment centers andinsertion companies) that might, in normal conditions, find it hard to obtain contracts, which in practice removes the contract from public competition, without however infringing the principles of free competition and nondiscrimination.

4. Technical capacity requirement: a certain technical solvency is demanded so that a tenderer's capacity can be evaluated, thereby determining whether they can be granted entry to compete; social aspects may be introduced when

---

126 What is more, it is expedient to do so, as it validates the later inclusion of procurement criteria or execution conditions of a social kind (Lesmes and Rodríguez, 2010: 45).

such an approach proves objective, proportionate, and reasonable given the nature and content of the contract.

5. Preference criteria: these are in place to deal with deadlock, contemplating social aspects associated with social, caring, nonprofit entities.

6. Procurement/assessment criterion: social criteria are applied at the evaluation stage for the different proposals, although this approach does prove to be the most restrictive.

7. Execution conditions: social criteria are set when the contract is performed, in the form of social obligations connected with the execution of the contract.

Since it is not legal to limit the access to public contracts to a specific legal form of enterprise (except for the reservation of contracts for insertion companies and special employment centers), the contract conditions shown above must be formulated so that social economy entities can turn their own assets[127] into competitive advantages (Moschitz 2004, 36), thereby encouraging participation from these bodies in public contracts. Indeed, "after a long time when the protection of competition policy was the mainstream in public markets the revision of the EU regulation of public procurement in 2014 (Directives 2014/23; 2014/24 and 2014/25) opened new opportunities to national, regional and local governments to foster social economy facilitating their access to public sector supplier status" (Monzon and Chaves 2017, 49).

---

127 For instance, integration of the obtaining of benefits for the community, a social return, in public procurement would increase the possibilities of social economy entities, but the contract is not reserved for them (Moschitz 2004, 37).

Other Measures Affecting the Activity of Entities, Grounded in the Manner of Regulation and of Operationalization of Partnerships between the Social Economy and the Public Administration

These are measures associated with the entities' activity, not as direct suppliers of the public administration, but rather as part of the public service supply, in relation with social welfare. Indeed, the welfare state is dependent on the social economy as an actor that is an executor of social welfare policies, offering services of social or general interest, and powerfully impacting upon the consolidation and development of the social economy (Monzón et al. 2009, 94–95). Formulas for offering such services can take shape in the following ways (Bakaikoa and Morandeira 2012, 252):

- Budgetary measures: budgetary items and/or programs designed to promote the activities of social economy entities, operationalized as subsidies, in which a distinction is drawn between subsidies following the ordinary procedure or by a competitive procedure, and subsidies based on special procedure or direct award procedure, generally by means of collaboration agreements.

- Agreement or contractualization: an instrument for formalizing the relation between the public administration and cooperatives, whereby the latter agree to supply a concrete service of social or general interest to the public.

- Service employment checks, vouchers, or coupons:[128] instruments that enable citizens to allocate the resources the state assigns them to the entity that offers the service that best satisfies or adapt to their needs, depending, in addition, on the public regulation governing entities capable of offering the service.

---

128 A detailed analysis of these tools can be consulted in Guillem López Casanovas (2003).

Public Policies Aimed at Employment in Social Economy Entities

These public policies aim directly at employment in the social economy or are general policies that benefit the social economy greatly; three kinds of measures can be identified, not all of which concentrate uniquely and exclusively on this sector of the economy (Chaves 2008, 56–59):

Support Measures for the Creation and Stabilization of Employment in the Social Economy

These are support programs for employment in the social economy, and they fall into the following categories:

- Aid for the direct creation of employment in social economy entities: Such aid favors the direct creation of employment through (partial or total) temporary subsidies for employees or by means of a reduction in workers' social welfare contributions.

- Aid for employment through incentives for the creation of a social economy entity: Such aid is normally associated with active employment policies and the most disadvantaged members of society or those at risk of social exclusion.

- Aid for the stabilization of employment in social economy entities: Aid for the preservation of employment, for the incorporation of employees as worker members or the incorporation of unemployed workers, especially those at risk of exclusion, as worker members in the social economy entity.

Support Measures for Social Economy Training

These measures consist of active employment policies addressed at labor force training and related to the creation of employment; they are generally horizontal, in that they are general nonspecific measures. Where the social and labor inclusion of the most disadvantaged groups or of those at risk of social exclusion are concerned, the entities normally adopt social economy approaches, taking part in the training of such groups to facilitate their integration in the ordinary job market. These social economy organizations thereby become active agents in applying active employment policies focusing on the precise sectors at whom specific measures are aimed.

Other measures

Worthy of note among other employment policy measures are steps taken to improve the match between the supply and demand of employment through the liberalization of employment services in private nonprofit agencies, or the adoption of temporary employment agency (known as Empresas de trabajo temporal or ETTs in Spain) forms of the social economy. Also of relevance are measures to stimulate the distribution of employment through social economy entities.

Conclusion

From an analysis of the theorization of public policies in the social economy, the following classification can be drawn, schematizing the different policies and resources, and identifying the promotion technique employed for each of them (See Table 5).

As can be observed, public policies for the advancement of the social economy break down into two large groups: soft policies, intended to establish an appropriate institutional and cultural environment, and hard policies, directed at the entities themselves, in their status as economic units and firms.

Table 6.5: Social Economy public policies, and promotion techniques

POLICIES aimed at Social Economy entities		Promotion activity techniques	
Supply policies (vis-à-vis the organizations' structure)			
Institutional measures	• Recognition of the Social Economy as a Private Actor and of its operational capacity in all sectors of economic activity. • Recognition of the Social Economy as a Political Actor. • Public bodies promoting the Social Economy	*Soft policies*	Legal Resources
Cognitive Measures	• Dissemination, training, and Social Economy research.	*Soft policies*	Direct E.R
Economic Measures	• Budgetary measures. • Fiscal measures. • Other financial support measures. • Technical support measures.	*Hard policies*	Direct E.R. Fiscal Resources Indirect E.R. Real resources
Demand policies (vis-à-vis the organizations' activity)			
	• Measures of access to the status of supplier to the Public Administration. • Measures of regulation and application of public-private partnerships with the Social Economy.	*Hard policies*	Direct economic resources Real resources
POLICIES aimed at employment in Social Economy entities			
	• Support measures for the creation and stabilization of employment in the Social Economy. • Support measures for Social Economy training. • Other measures.	*Hard policies* Legal Resources	Direct E. R.

Source: Morandeira (2013: 194).

It must be noted that the type of public promotion policies that are taken will depend, to a great degree, on the conception that the policymakers have of the sector; that is, on whether they consider the social economy to be a collective objective per se, capable of constituting a desirable social and economic model; or whether they regard it as an instrument for attaining other collective goals, becoming an intermediate objective.

Thus, the main social economy promotion techniques are seen to be measures of an economic kind. Here, subsidies have the greatest presence.

Meanwhile, where institutional legal resources are concerned, integration of the recognition of the social economy as a private actor and of recognition of the operational capacity of the social economy within any sector of economic activity as one and the same measure is regarded as appropriate, since both measures are linked with juridical/legal aspects affecting the social economy and its activity. And recognition of the sector as a political actor is justified because of the important position the social economy holds within the socioeconomic reality of society, making it necessary to include it in the political process.

In any event, even if more economic measures are identified in the theoretical sense, their types and intensities will depend upon the competences of the various levels of public players and the stance they adopt toward the social economy.

Bibliography

Bakaikoa, Baleren, and Jon Morandeira. 2012. "El cooperativismo vasco y las políticas públicas." *Ekonomiaz-Revista Vasca de Economía* 79: 234–63.

Chaves, Rafael. 2002. "Politiques Publiques et Economie Sociale en Europe: le cas de l'Espagne." *Annals of Public and Cooperative Economics* 73: 3: 453–80.

————. 2008. "Public Policies and Social Economy in Spain and
Europe." *CIRIEC-España-Revista de Economía Pública, Social y
Cooperativa* 62: 35–60.

————. 2010. "Las actividades de cobertura institucional: infraestruc-
turas de apoyo y políticas públicas de fomento de la Economía
Social." In *La Economía Social en España en el Año 2008. Ámbito,
magnitudes, actividades y tendencias*, edited by Jose Luis Monzón.
Valencia: CIRIEC-España.

————. 2012. "Las políticas públicas y las cooperativas." *Ekonomiaz-
Revista Vasca de Economía* 79: 168–96.

Chaves, Rafael, and Jose Luis Monzón. 2000. "Políticas Públicas." In
Economía Social y Empleo en la Unión Europea, edited by Rafael
Chaves, Danièle Demoustier, Jose Luis Monzón, Enzzo Pezzi-
ni, Roger Spear, and Bernad Thiry. Valencia. CIRIEC-España.

Fonfría, Antonio. 2006. *Un análisis taxonómico de las políticas para pyme en
Europa: objetivos, instrumentos y empresas beneficiarias*. Papeles de
trabajo del Instituto de Estudios Fiscales. Madrid: Instituto de
Estudios Fiscales.

Lesmes, Santiago. 2008. *Guía de Contratación Pública Sostenible. Incorporación de Criterios Sociales*. Córdoba: IDEAS.

Lesmes, Santiago, and Laura Rodriguez. 2010. *Guía de Contratación
Pública Sostenible. Incorporación de Criterios Sociales*. Córdoba:
IDEAS.

López Casanovas, Guillem, ed. 2003. *Los nuevos instrumentos de gestión
pública*. Colección de Estudios 31. Barcelona: Servicios de
Estudios la Caixa.

Monzón, Jose Luis, Rafael Calvo, Rafael Chaves, Isabel Gemma Fajardo, and Fernando Valdés. 2009. *Informe para la Elaboración de
una Ley de Fomento de la Economía Social*. Valencia: CIRIEC.

Monzón, Jose Luis, and Rafael Chaves, eds. 2017. *Recent Evolutions of the
Social Economy in the European Union*. Brussels: European Economic and Social Committee.

Moschitz, Silke. 2004. *Guía CARPE de compra responsable.* Brussels: Ciudades Europeas por el Consumo Responsable.

Morandeira, Jon. 2013. *El servicio público de fomento de la Economía Social en el País Vasco desde una perspectiva de orientación al mercado. Propuestas y acciones.* Donostia-San Sebastián: Universidad del País Vasco/ Euskal Herriko Unibertsitatea.

Savall, Teresa. 2013. "Análisis de la participación de la economía social en el diálogo social." *Revista Vasca de Economía Social* 9: 111–41.

Vaillancourt, Yves. 2009. "Social Economy in the Co-construction of Public Policy." *Annals of Public and Cooperative Economics* 80, no. 2: 275–313.

7

Politics at Work: Worker Cooperatives and Territorial Mobilizations in the French Basque Country[129]

XABIER ITÇAINA

The study of worker cooperatives provides food for thought in the ongoing interdisciplinary dialogue between political sociology and economic sociology. Contrary to what is generally assumed by the neoclassical perspective, the evaluation of economic actors' interests is often combined with other more binding motivations that partake in morals, social responsibility, feelings, trust, and social links; competition is a subsystem embedded in a societal context, made up of values, power, and social relations (Caillé 1990). According to

---

129 This chapter relies on empirical material collected during several Sciences Po Bordeaux – Aquitaine Region research programs (Gouvernance locale et développement économique territorial, 2004–2007; Vers une gouvernance transfrontalière en réseau? Expériences transfrontalières d'économie sociale au Pays basque et en Irlande, 2010–2014; ESSAQUI-Institutionnalisations en miroir de l'économie sociale et solidaire en Aquitaine - 2015–2019). The author thanks Aitor Bengoetxea and GEZKI for their invitation, Jean-François Allafort and Dave Passingham for their help in translating this chapter, and Andy Smith for his comments.

the "new economic sociology" (DiMaggio 1994), culture may not be the sole factor structuring economic behavior and institutions, but it is instrumental in shaping them: "Culture can affect economic behavior by influencing how actors define their interests (*constitutive effects* . . .) by constraining their efforts on their own behalf (*regulatory* effects), or by shaping a group's capacity to mobilize, or its goal in mobilizing" (DiMaggio 1994, 28).

This epistemological position is fruitful for the analysis of the influence of territorial cultures and identities on local development politics and can lead to at least three types of research design. The first is focused on the conceptualization of culture and identity in regional and territorial policy-making (Palard 2009; Syssner 2009). The second is centered on the analysis of a sector of activity with a view to discovering how territory impacts upon "political work" within such spaces (Smith 2008). The third approach addresses a well-determined type of firm, in a manner similar to that of social economy specialists, and discusses interactions between this organizational model and the sociopolitical and economic dynamics of the territory (Demoustier 2004).

This third option will be followed here, through a territorial case study. Despite its obvious limits, I contend here that such a research design enables us to disentangle the aggregate interlock of cultural, economic, and sociopolitical factors on a given territory. This article tries to apprehend this puzzle through qualitative research on worker cooperatives in the French Basque region.[130]There are three reasons

---

130 A first qualitative survey was conducted by the author, together with G. Guillat and Sébastien Ségas, in 2004–2006 on fifteen worker cooperatives in the French Basque Country. Interviews were conducted with managers, CEOs, and financial directors of SCOPs (sociétés cooperatives ouvrières de production, worker cooperatives). In 2004, the author also attended the regular meetings of the Sorlan association, whose objective was to foster cooperativism in the French Basque Country. The study was complemented by interviews with the SCOP Regional Union and the CRESS (Chambre régionale de l'économie sociale et solidaire, Regional social and solidarity economy chamber) Aquitaine, and by several visits to Mondragón. This data was updated in 2010–2013 on a cross-border basis in the French and Spanish Basque regions and in the framework of the ESSAQUI research program on the institutionalization of the social economy in the Aquitaine region (2015–2019) (see note above).

for this focus on a small territory – the French Basque Country refers to the Basque-speaking western part (290,000 inhabitants in 2008) of the Pyrénées-Atlantiques department on the Franco-Spanish border. First, this territory has been affected by a significant worker cooperatives movement since the mid-1970s, a fact that singles it out in the French context. Second, as it is directly inspired by the Mondragón experience, the French Basque cooperative movement finely illustrates the virtues and the difficulties involved in exportation of the Southern Basque model.

Third, the political dimension was a crucial factor in the genesis and further development of the French Basque cooperative movement. The main assumption here is that the French Basque worker cooperatives may be regarded as an organized form of representation of a wider territory and identity-based social movement. This process was first to be found in the highly politicized genesis of the cooperative movement in the 1970s–1980s. In its early stage, the Basque cooperative movement contributed to transforming local economic development into a public and a political issue, and to setting the issue on the local governmental agenda. Nevertheless, the cooperative movement has evolved from a highly politicized genesis to a more pragmatic stance signaled both by adjustments to market conditions and by a reinforced partnership with the actors of territorial governance. On this last point, cooperatives benefited in the 1990s–2000s from changes in the French legal regulatory framework for cooperatives, from the new participative territorial governance in the French Basque Country, and from the cross-border opportunities offered by European integration.

This chapter is structured as follows: It begins by briefly reviewing the two shortcomings in the academic literature that this case-study aims at addressing. It then turns to the case-study and addresses the original politico-territorial matrix that gave birth to the worker cooperatives movement in the 1970s–1980s. Therafter, it addresses the adaptation of this alternative organizational and sociopolitical model to market constraints and to changing forms of territorial governance. The concluding section puts in perspective the French

Basque case with regard to the more general discussion on politics of/in cooperativism and makes suggestions for further research.

Politics at Work: Territorial Identity, Cooperativism, and Social Movements

The objective of this chapter is thus to tentatively address two deficits or shortcomings in academic literature. The first of these, as highlighted by Michael Keating, John Loughlin, and Kris Deschouwer (2003, 19), concerns the political economy of the new regional cultural movements. Whereas much research has been conducted on their political dimension *stricto sensu*—party and electoral competition, political violence, and identity politics—the economic dimension of subnational mobilizations has not been much explored to date. Interestingly, research has been conducted on how classifications of regional culture and identity take shape in a context in which regional competitiveness has become the main goal for regional politicians. Relying on cases in the Swedish and German regions, Josefina Syssner finds, for instance, that the understanding of regions as competitors in the global race for economic growth has brought with it a stereotypification, commodification, and stratification of categories such as "regional culture" and "regional identity" (2009, 439). Thus, a lot remains to be done to cross-cut such analysis of elite interpretations of regional identity with observation of territorial and community uses of collective identity in the economic field. This field of research may prove very promising through a study of the links between culture, territory, and the economy, combining a grassroots approach and an approach more focused on institutional economics and politics (Bekemans 1998).[131]

This bias is particularly sensitive in the French Basque case. Even though they have been less studied than their Southern coun-

---

131 Taken separately, the first approach lays too much stress on the community dimension and isolates local initiatives from market mechanisms, whereas the second focus, mainly centered on post-Fordist production systems (industrial districts, an urban economy of services, and high technology), tends to give exclusive importance to regional success stories (Bekemans 1989)

terparts, the French Basque territorial mobilizations have received renewed attention over the last few years. However, this attention has been biased toward political and institutional processes, neglecting more "discrete" socioeconomic mobilizations. Research has been conducted on an historical account of Basque nationalism (Jacob 1994), sociopolitical activism among young French Basques (Bray 2006), and political claims for a separate Basque *département* (Chaussier 2002; Mansvelt Beck 2005). More specifically, Igor Ahedo (2005) points out the contrast between the weak electoral showing of nationalism in the French Basque Country, and its role in the territorial institutionalization process and strength in the cultural and economic spheres. In line with his observation, the objective of the present chapter is to shift the focus of research from the institutional systems and the nationalist movements toward more discrete forms of mobilization in the field of economics, which cannot simply be reduced to the nationalist/nonnationalist categories. Zoe Bray is right when expressing doubts about "the usage of the term ethnonational for describing all grassroots political mobilizations in places like the Basque Country" (Bray 2006, 534). One can only explain the logics of collective action in the economic field by grasping the complex relationships between sector-based interests, plural references to territorial identities, and permanent adaptation to the changing institutional and market environment. Indeed, this approach is not only particularly relevant for the analysis of Basque farmers' mobilizations (Itçaina 2009; Itçaina and Gomez 2015), but also in the case of the social economy and worker cooperatives. If we adopt Keating, Loughlin, and Deschouwer's (2003, 36) distinctions on the notions of regional or territorial identity (cognitive, affective, and instrumental), we uphold the hypothesis that the French Basque worker cooperative movement relies on an *instrumental* approach to territorial identity (territory used as a basis for mobilization and collective action), mixed with an *affective* sense of belonging (how it provides a framework for common identity and solidarity, possibly in competition with other forms of identity such as class or nation).

The second deficit concerns the cooperatives themselves. Even though social economy and third sector experiences have received increasing attention from political sociology over the last decade, most research work has focused, strictly speaking, on the associative sectors and on nonprofit bodies. Worker cooperatives, which belong to the more market-oriented social economy sectors, have indeed been neglected in the most restrictive approaches to the third sector.[132] This relative silence contrasts with the well-known intense debate between economists and socioeconomists on the efficiency of the cooperative firm. Nevertheless, political sociology has a lot to say about these experiences. Cooperatives have a political dimension for at least four reasons. First, their corporate culture is based on highly political management principles: free membership, internal democracy, social or community responsibility, and resource mix. Second, this set of values is historically grounded on political cultures and a variety of ideological sources (George 1997). Third, cooperatives have both seminal and structuring relations with the territory: setting up a cooperative means creating local jobs, maintaining capital in the territory, and furthering a relatively endogenous and/ or bottom-up vision of economic development. The embeddedness of cooperatives is frequently associated with territorialized political cultures. Regions from the "Third Italy" are well-known for the overlapping of the cooperative movement and territorial "red" and "white" political cultures (Menzani 2007). Closer to my case-study, the emblematic Spanish Basque cooperative system of Mondragón, associating cooperatives with industrial, consumer, banking, mutual benefit, and training missions, has also been approached as a political experience by authors who have focused either on the ideas (Christian personalism and work ethics) of Mondragón's founders (Azurmendi 1984), on the transformation of these values (Azkarraga 2007; Cheney 2002), or on the debate generated by cooperativism among leftist and Basque nationalist milieus (Kasmir 1996). Fourth, cooperatives can happen to furnish an organizational form

---

132 Salamon and Anheier (1995) include in the *nonprofit sector* organizations presenting a formal constitution, a legally private status, the presence of a form of self-government, the nonredistribution of profits, and the presence of volunteers. According to Jean-Louis Laville (2000), the volunteer status condition may exclude sectors of the traditional social economy, such as worker cooperatives and mutuals, which can redistribute profit to their members in a limited way and are founded in the name of general and/or mutual interest.

promoted and legitimized by social movements (Soule 2012, 1717). Social movements can also choose to "invest" in cooperatives, that is, in economic mobilization, in which political access is blocked or political means are rejected as in the case of anticorporate movements in the US in the late nineteenth and early twentieth centuries (Schneiberg, King, and Smith 2008). Drawing on their fieldwork on a cooperatively owned mine in South Wales (Tower Colliery), Len Arthur et al. (2004) consider that worker cooperatives, which are significantly different from typical work organizations, can be considered as *social movements* that generate specific contentious social spaces. Karen Ann Faulk (2008) examines the rise of cooperativism in Argentina through the ethnographic analysis of the Bauen hotel, a worker cooperative supported by a social movement that seeks to delegitimize the cultural conceptions implicit in neoliberalism. Likewise, I believe that the genesis and transformation of the worker cooperatives movement in the French Basque Country provide a good encounter of both the debates over the political economy of regionalism and the political dimension of cooperativism.

Genesis: Territorial Activism, Crises, and Opportunities

As noted, then, I will first examine the original politico-territorial matrix that gave birth to the worker cooperatives movement in the 1970s and 1980s.

Militant genesis

The new wave[133] of French Basque worker cooperatives in the 1970s–1980s originated in a five-dimensional matrix. In ideological

---

133 Previous cooperative experiences displayed distinct ideological backgrounds. A cooperative printing house founded in Baiona (Bayonne) in 1905—the oldest SCOP in Aquitaine—is an example of an alliance between anarcho-syndicalism and a family-owned firm, with no reference to Basque identity. Similarly, in the 1930s, a worker cooperative was founded by sandal makers

terms, to begin with, the concept of self-management progressively became central to the economic doctrine of the *abertzale* (Basque nationalist) movement. The *Enbata* political movement that had evolved in the early 1970s—as had its Spanish Basque counterpart—from a Christian-Democrat legacy to left-wing nationalism (Jacob 1994) stands out in particular. The second influence came from the French worker cooperatives movement. The number of SCOPs (French legal status for worker cooperatives) increased in the 1970s and 1980s, when self-management was promoted by some trade-unions (such as the CFDT, Confédération Française du Travail, French Workers' Confederation) and left-wing parties (the PSU, Parti Socialiste Unifié, Unified Socialist Party, in particular). In third place, there was the indirect influence of religion mediated through a mix of doctrinal references to social Catholicism (when promoting the cooperative model as an alternative solution halfway between socialism and capitalism), culture (a traditional form of mistrust of the state and a bias toward self-government and self-management), and institutions (the role of denominational schools and of Catholic Action in the propagation of the cooperative idea in the 1960s and 1970s). The fourth factor was constituted by cultural predispositions toward cooperation inherited from customary reciprocity systems. In that respect, the founders of the first worker cooperatives whom we interviewed referred repeatedly to their own peasant origins and established a parallel between customary institutions of mutual help between neighbors (*auzolan*), the use of common lands, and the collective dimension of cooperativism; and the customary regime of farm transmission and indivisible shares in the cooperative firm.[134]

---

and promoted by the leftist CGT (Confédération Générale du Travail, General Workers' Union) union in the small industrial city of Maule (Mauléon). The first fishermen's cooperatives were also founded by the CGT in 1916 in Donibane Lohizune (Saint-Jean-de-Luz). Farmers' cooperatives, by contrast, were profoundly marked by social Catholicism.

134 The economist François Fourquet insists on this fourth dimension in the province of Zuberoa (Soule), without overestimating it: a predisposition toward debate with a view to reaching agreements on the model of the *artzain-bideka* (a customary law among shepherds who convene before each season to determine the respective part of each in the enterprise); attachment to the *etxaltia* (house) and the *premü* common law (the advantage given to the chosen heir by both brothers and sisters, against payment of the *etxaltia*); the

Although partly idealized, this reference played a role in orienting these activists toward the cooperative as an organizational model. The fifth and crucial factor was the cross-border influence of the Spanish Basque cooperative experience of Mondragón.

Learning from the South

Learning from Mondragón was essential to the creation of the first SCOPs in the French Basque Country which initially specialized in two main sectors: electrical equipment and furniture. Copelec, an electric wiring cooperative founded in 1975, was the first concrete emanation of Partzuer, an association created in 1974 for the promotion of cooperatives. Likewise, Alki, a furniture factory, was set up in 1982 by four young French Basques on their return from a long sojourn in the Mondragón cooperatives in the late 1970s.

The trajectory of one of Alki's founding members is highly significant with regard to the double—cooperative *and* political—socialization received by French Basques at Mondragón. After graduating in mechanical engineering in Bordeaux, P. U.[135] contacted Partzuer, which directed him to Mondragón. "The objective was to send us there after graduating from university, in connection with the *abertzale* movement, so that we could do something here after coming back home."[136] The socialization process was progressive: P. U. started as a cleaning operative who worked around the clock in eight-hour shifts. He stayed for six months in a factory before spending two and a half years in a clerical position. He progressively became familiar with "the atmosphere of the workplace" but also

tradition of the valley assembly (*silviet*) under the modern form of a general assembly for development planning, and the customary collective management of the *cayolar* (the collective production unit of mountain shepherds) (Fourquet 1998, 98). Concerning Zuberoa again, Kepa Fernández de Larrinoa (2009) observes a continuity between the customary institutions of shepherds for the collective management of summer pastures and the production of milk and cheese (*olha*), and a new cooperative that was designed to facilitate cheese production and, above all, marketing.

135 These initials are used to preserve the interviewee's anonymity.
136 Interview, translated from Basque.

with the local culture and the "atmosphere of a highly politicized society." "Everything was mixed together," professional socialization and political training in a country then caught up in the turmoil of the democratic transition. P. U. became a member of the furniture cooperative that belonged to the Ularcop group with eight other cooperatives, including Fagor elecrodomésticos, the driving force behind the whole cooperative movement. This young French Basque also discovered the large-scale collective decision-making processes:

There was a big meeting, in which everybody had to pay something. A contribution to the firm's capital. Between all the eight thousand workers, from different factories. For everybody or nothing at all. Then there was a vote and that was it. We gave the equivalent of two months' salary. That was big. Such solidarity between all factory workers. We helped each other, we had to put in money, and everybody agreed. Eight thousand people, not just eighty. That was a strong force for facing up to the future.[137]

Far from providing just inspiration, Mondragón was also directly involved in the further development of French Basque cooperatives. The furniture SCOP Denek ("all together") was created in Arrosa (Saint-Martin d'Arrossa, Lower Navarre) in 1979. Transborder solidarity was strong as the Mondragón cooperatives decided to give financial help to Denek, after a general assembly decision. Caja Laboral, the Mondragón cooperative bank, became a financial partner and Mondragón proposed the services of a specialist who would be in charge of the development of the cooperatives in the French Basque Country. But transfers of capital were made impossible on account of political and administrative constraints. Amid mounting public protest and demonstrations against such administrative obstacles, the survival of Denek became a matter of public concern.

The idea of complementary production lines gave rise to the creation of many subcontracting companies. As Denek had to import chairs, five young entrepreneurs decided to set up Alki, a furniture cooperative, in the village of Itsasu (Itxassou) in 1982. Market research was conducted, and a financing plan was established on the model

_____

137 Ibid.

of the Mondragón bank. The French SCOP movement supported the project. Alki started production with forty workers, a manager, and a supervisory board. Technical expertise and cooperative culture were very low, but that was compensated for by strong activism, enhanced by the presence of a Southern Basque political refugee who was a former engineer from Mondragón. Each cooperative member brought 15,000 francs worth of capital, a significantly high amount of money, especially for young activists-cum-entrepreneurs:

Maybe we didn't really think much about the whole business from the start. We really wanted to make something out of it. There was a kind of innocent enthusiasm. Then we were helped, there was something concrete to back us up. There was that atmosphere. Things started moving everywhere. We were into the movement. And there was also technical backing. We couldn't have done anything alone. In our group, nobody had ever made a single chair. We knew just a little about woodwork. I had just spent a year in Denek. We knew nothing about production or selling. Everything had to be created from scratch. . . . We were almost forty at the start. Because of the Mondragón production model. Then we became aware that we were too many. Forty people and nobody who could make a chair! . . . The local youth expected much from us. But we had to explain that they had to pay in order to work. That was quite revolutionary. Yes, it was because the factory belonged to each of us.[138]

A Failed Process of Integration

The Mondragón model, however, implied a process of inter-co-operative integration. Indeed, taking their inspiration from the Mondragón model, the French Basque cooperatives created Lana as a coordinating body in 1982. Despite its eventual failure, Lana was the perfect example of the value system the French Basque cooperative movement was based on. In the eyes of its promoters, the cooperative movement was first and foremost a social movement, as exemplified in the statutes of Lana:

---

138 Ibid.

The ideal objective of the workers' production cooperatives of the Basque Country is to change the job market in the region; its short-term objective is to improve
workers' conditions through cooperation and their
control over the management of the firms. As a response
to the workers' expectations, the cooperatives aim at
transferring the means of production and exchange
to the workers so that they can fully take part in the
decision-making process that is essential to the future
of the producers. They intend thereby to prove the full
capacity of the workers in economic matters and train
them for their future tasks. They are gathered in an association called "Lana" whose objective is to represent
the *Basque Cooperative Movement* and help them achieve
this objective, directly or indirectly, through its own
services or through distinct organizations, companies,
groups, or unions of cooperatives and cooperators.[139]

This political objective was reflected in the efforts made to create a genuine cooperative socialization process. To join the Lana
association, each SCOP had to meet the following requirements:

Each member SCOP must have statutes in conformity with the standard statutes as established by Lana
or acknowledged by Lana as being in conformity
with the cooperative principles of the Lana cooperative movement and with the legislation in force.

Each member SCOP must undertake to respect the
basic principles of the Lana cooperative movement:

All workers are members of the cooperative and each member is a worker.

Creation of a community fund

External solidarity regarding wages (the average SCOP wages must be equal to the average wages in Lana's zone of influence)

---

139 Statutes of the Lana association, translated from French (private archives).

Internal solidarity regarding wages (wages range from 1 to 3)

Systematic reinvestment of the profits generated by the workforce

A commitment to abide by all the rules as established in Lana's rules and regulations

Each SCOP must be represented by at least two Lana active members.[140]

This social movement dimension was also noticeable among cooperative experiences that added new societal concerns—such as environmentalism—to the territorial motivation. The genesis of Loreki followed this logic. Founded in July 1985 in Itsasu (Lapurdi/Labourd), this SCOP was created *ex nihilo* by four young activists after a two-year-long feasibility study carried out by the Ekhindar ("solar energy") association. Their idea was to exploit organic resources and thus create local jobs. The association was composed of forty members who all came from the French Basque Country and were fully trained engineers or salespeople. One group specialized in renewable energies while another focused on the potential use of recycled waste in agriculture. Thanks to 390,000 francs worth of subsidies and 10,000 francs of self-financing, the association hired three full-time employees in 1984 whose task was to conduct a feasibility study. The firm was not only helped by Herrikoa ("from/for the people")—a local venture capital firm launched in 1980 by the *abertzale* movement—but also by the local, departmental, and regional authorities, together with the Ministry of the Environment. The wider public was also invited to participate in the firm's financing plan. Indeed, between 40,000 and 50,000 francs worth of promissory loans were collected during the annual festival, Lapurtarren biltzarra ("gathering of the Lapurdi people"). Industrial issues were politicized and transformed into collective and public issues.

Most local SCOPs were created *ex nihilo*. This, added to the ideological matrix, may explain why labor unions played a relatively minor role in the Basque cooperative movement, in comparison with

---

140 Article 7, Lana Statutes.

what occurred in the Béarn part of the department. However, the same activist logic was to be found in the few cooperatives (such as this electrical equipment SCOP in Hazparne [Hasparren]) which originated from the buy-out of a failing company. Their founding members clearly defined themselves as "activists," using the cooperative status so they could "live and work here in our country."[141]

Fundraising campaigns, the strong presence of Spanish Basque political refugees in French Basque SCOPs, public demonstrations, and Basque nationalist discourse: the foundation of cooperatives was inherently politicized. The blurred frontiers between public and private action illustrated a three-fold protest movement that engaged in campaigning against conventional business managerial models, against the apathy of local and national authorities over local economic development, but also against a Basque movement deemed too culturalist and exclusively focused on institutional claims. In the minds of the founding fathers of the cooperative movement, territorial identity was perceived as a positive resource for economic development, thus challenging the mere symbolic use of the Basque image for territorial marketing (Lougarot 2005).

Varieties of Cooperativism

However, the activist approach did not apply unanimously and univocally to all the Basque SCOPs. Extensive internal democracy was sometimes perceived as an obstacle to the management of the firm, as exemplified by a cooperative in the province of Zuberoa, specialized in the production of steel frames, which was founded in 1983 by five employees who had bought out a liquidated company. They considered themselves a somewhat atypical cooperative, with a rather low membership rate (around 20 percent). Its founding managers regarded any extended participation and internal democracy as a permanent threat: "Many SCOPs collapsed because of internal problems. Old scores were settled. Some people got fired. Some members have got this idea firmly fixed in their minds. They think

---

141 Interview, Hazparne.

that if they take on new people, and if there are problems one day, they may well be laid-off."[142]

Likewise, in several small-sized SCOPs, of more recent creation, ideological references were more diffuse. In some cases, SCOP status was even a purely utilitarian choice, principally due to the tax break granted to such firms. Links with the territory could also be essentially functional and instrumental. The pragmatic dimension of the cooperative movement as a solution to the crises that took place in the 1970s and 1980s should not be overlooked. Nevertheless, several other examples show that references to the values attached to the cooperative movement were maintained, but in a somewhat confused or diffused way. Several SCOPs were created by the promoters of older and bigger cooperatives, founded on ideological grounds, which had however gone bankrupt – as in the case of a computer engineering firm established in 1991 by former workers from a bigger cooperative, in which references to the "Mondragón tutelage," "the spirit of cooperation," and the "desire to live and work in the Basque country"[143] were mixed with more pragmatic fiscal and financial considerations.

A New Set of References? Cooperatives, Markets, and New Territorial Governance

The matrix of values that was discussed above may be aptly used to describe the emergence and initial development of the French Basque cooperative movement. It contributes to explain the importance of

---

142 Interview, Maule. An organizational culture approach (DiMaggio 1994) could help to assess how principles are implemented. Socioeconomists who have analyzed twelve SCOPs in the Rhône-Alpes region have come up with four profiles characterized either by a *cooperation logic* that tentatively tries to reconcile job protection, professional qualification, and internal democracy; by a *professional logic* focused on professional autonomy and qualification; by an *industrial logic* in which job protection prevails; or by a *financial logic* when the weight of the financers may lead the companies toward job instrumentalization, or when subsidiaries are used to increase the value of work and yield (Cassier et al. 2003).

143 Interview, Baiona.

the Basque cooperative movement at the Aquitaine regional level.[144] But a cultural and/or ideological approach does not fully account for the second period in the history of the movement, when cooperatives were confronted with changes in the market and in their sociopolitical environment. After the highly ideological 1970s and 1980s came a period when the worker cooperatives questioned and challenged their founding utopian tenets. The religious references disappeared, except as an implicit reference to an ethic of work and sharing. The initial nationalist/regionalist profession of faith of the cooperative managers was progressively replaced by a more pluralistic feeling of territorial belonging, a form of attachment to *some* of its specificities—notably the Basque language—and a critical approach to identity-based types of mobilizations that had neglected the economic dimension.

Values Tested by the Markets

The economic constraints created by new sectional circumstances and globalized markets had a deep impact on cooperatives and could undermine their approach to territorial development. This was particularly the case for cooperatives that were fully integrated in highly competitive sectors of production. Cooperatives, here as elsewhere, were simultaneously "straddling the divide between employee ownership and control and operating within a framework dominated by capitalist market relations" (Arthur et al. 2004, 1). As

---

144 In 2017, the Pyrénées-Atlantiques département ranked second in (the old) Aquitaine (it ranked first in 2010) in terms of the number of worker cooperatives (SCOPs and SCICs), with 45 out of a total of 146. Moreover, 31 (28 in 2010) worker cooperatives were located in the Basque Country and 14 (11 in 2010) in Béarn, despite the fact that Béarn is more highly populated than the Basque Country. Membership rates were markedly high. French Basque SCOPs are rather small-sized firms (between 2 and 92 workers, representing an average of 18 per cooperative) and are involved in various sectors: printing, electrical and telephone equipment, electronic wiring, fertilizers, pharmaceuticals, industrial casting and molding, furniture, services and trade, media, and culture (URSCOP Aquitaine, http://www.scop-aquitaine.coop/sites/fr/unions-regionales/les-scop-aquitaine/, consulted on December 19, 2017).

early as the 1980s, the economic crisis soon heightened competition among cooperatives that operated in the same sectors of activity.

The crisis that affected the market in the early 1980s strained the partnership between Alki and Denek, which would otherwise have paved the way for an integration process in the cooperative movement. Half of Alki's production was initially sold to Denek. But the two factories progressively adopted diverging strategies. Alki started to look for new outlets and boost its commercial activities. New management decisions were made to adjust working time to production requirements and costs. Alki's workers decided to work overtime for free. It was also necessary to increase capital, and in 1983 the initial individual outlay was doubled, which led to the departure of about ten members. The destiny of Alki took on a wider public dimension. In 1984, Herrikoa launched a fund-raising campaign throughout the Basque Country. A total of 1,300,000 francs was collected from the public, with half the sum destined to Alki, which was also financially helped by conventional banks. Conversely, the situation of Denek worsened because of the crisis and because the necessary managerial decisions were not made in time. It was not enough to train cooperative activists; professional entrepreneurs were also necessary. Cooperation between Alki and Denek rapidly turned into competition.

The bankruptcy of Denek in 1985 was a symbol that affected the whole cooperative movement, and the initial utopian objectives were put to the test. Out of the three SCOPs respectively created in the provinces of Lapurdi (Alki), Lower Navarre (Denek), and Zuberoa (Orhi), only one survived. Alki successfully recovered from the crisis. Its financial situation, in deficit until 1985–86, significantly improved after 1987.[145] However, the failure of Denek brought about the end of Lana as an experience of inter-cooperation that had originally been founded on the Alki-Denek partnership.

---

145 Indeed, since 2004, Alki had a stronger position in the sector of furniture production in France, which, regardless of cultural and political proximity, was not the case in the Spanish Basque Country because its products were not adapted to the Spanish market.

There was no longer any flagship firm that could act as the driving force behind the movement. The same phenomenon happened in the 1990s to SEI, a computer service and maintenance firm. A leader in Aquitaine, SEI embodied this new generation of high-tech firms, in contrast to the more traditional activities of the small-sized SCOPs. SEI was first created as a public limited company in 1976 and became a cooperative in the 1980s. After its initial success, this fast-developing firm had to file for bankruptcy in 1993, which was a severe blow to the whole cooperative movement in the region (Larralde 2007). Paradoxically enough, the firm was eventually acquired by the Mondragón group, but did not keep its cooperative status. There were new attempts of inter-cooperation afterward, but on a significantly different model from Lana, notably with Obeki, an association set up by former SEI workers to reinforce the training of cooperators. Furthermore, after the failure of Denek, cooperation with Mondragón slackened in the French Basque Country during the severe crisis that hit the Spanish Basque cooperative corporation in 1990 and 1991. The various SCOPs had to adjust to market change, notably by starting to subcontract their production.

The local influence of these global trends can be highlighted through the case of O.,[146] an industrial molding and casting factory, which was established in Lapurdi in 1980 by a self-employed manager. Specializing initially in high-precision mechanical engineering, then in thermoplastic injection mold-making, it became a worker cooperative in 1984. This cooperative was influenced by self-management ideology and Basque nationalism. The industrial plan of O. was itself conceived from the broader political perspective of economic development of the Basque rural hinterland through industrialization, in close partnership with the Spanish Basque Country. Three skilled engineers, who had fled the Spanish Basque Country for political reasons, were hired. The economic crisis in the mid-1990s led to streamlining decisions. Indeed, O. depended heavily on the Spanish market and was directly hit by the 30 percent devaluation of the peseta in 1992, which led to higher inflation in Spain. The company was no longer competitive; its prices were 30

---

146 This initial is used to preserve the firm's anonymity.

percent too high. It then decided to look for new outlets, especially in West Africa, with the help of French oil and gas company Total. In 1998, the Maier group, a subsidiary of Mondragón set up in Gernika, placed a first order. Commercial contacts were facilitated by the presence of a young French Basque engineer in Gernika. Trust based on calculation and information exchange added to trust based on shared identity and values (Harrisson 2003). In 2003–4, around 45 percent of O.'s business volume was generated through Maier. In a globalized market, O. considered extending its commercial activities in Algeria, though it refused to outsource its production unit. Product specialization became the condition necessary to diversify its local market and work nation-wide in France and in Spain. International constraints also challenged the validity of the cooperative formula, notably where outsourcing of the productive process was concerned.[147] O.'s manager then had to cope with internal debates over the cooperative model. While difficulties engendered by the collective decision-making process may frequently urge some SCOPs to resort to traditional management techniques (Huntzinger 1994), here it was rather the lack of participation of workers in decision-making and the emergence of a "trade union mentality"[148] that O.'s manager deplored. Amid increasing economic difficulties, O. then tried to reactivate the political and territorial dimension of the cooperative project by issuing shares in 2004. By so doing, O. wanted to involve the local community in this project, thus turning the destiny of the company into a public issue, as the pioneer cooperatives had done in the 1980s.

---

147 In 2000, Maier had to set up a production unit in Lichfield, in the UK, to be as close as possible to the customers. It gave rise to controversy over the status of the workers—single wage-earners or full members of the cooperative?—in the UK (Tremlett 2001) and in the Spanish Basque Country, as several cooperators in Gernika were reluctant to go and work in Lichfield.
148 Interview, O.'s manager.

Cooperatives and New Territorial Governance: From Alternative to Partnership

Simultaneously, the relations between the cooperative movement and territorial policy-making experienced a marked change. In the 1970s, Basque worker cooperatives claimed they could offer an alternative to the assumed apathy of local and national authorities in matters of local development. But this *protest* logic seems to have given way progressively to a *partnership* approach. This change resulted from the conjunction of three factors.

First, changes in the French legal regulation of the social economy opened up new opportunities for cooperatives, after several decades of slowing down. The Basque cooperative movement had initially benefited from the state policies in favor of worker cooperatives initiated in the late 1970s. The July 19, 1978 Law on SCOPs particularly facilitated the creation of worker cooperatives by lowering the required minimum amount of capital and minimum number of members (from seven to two). However, in the following decade, public support for the social economy shifted from the cooperative to the associative sector. While the status of cooperatives had been seen until then as an essential tool for combating both unemployment *and* social exclusion, state level policy-makers soon came to realize that encouraging companies to be competitive was difficult to reconcile with the employment of unqualified personnel. Unskilled workers were thus to be looked after by new *associative* bodies that had developed in the field of social integration (Demoustier 2001). In the French Basque Country, the slowing down of cooperative creation in the 1990s was accompanied by the creation of a significant number of associations in the field of social integration, but also in the cultural, environmental, and socio-educative sectors. In the 2000s, however, there was renewed interest in the cooperative formula from associations looking for a status that better fitted their professional activities. New legal opportunities, notably the SCIC,[149] created in 2001 (Law 2001-624) on the model of Italian

---

149 Société Coopérative d'Intérêt Collectif (Collective Interest Cooperative Society).

social cooperatives, allowed multi-stakeholder partnerships between cooperative firms and private and public partners on an inter-sectoral basis, without being limited to social integration. Actors belonging to the Basque social economy, such as the associative TV channel Aldudarrak Bideo in Lower Navarre and a market-gardening company in Lapurdi, endorsed this new cooperative status to institutionalize their partnership with local authorities.

Second, cooperatives became involved in the new multilevel territorial governance of the Basque Country, which had become more open to partnerships between civil society and policymakers. From the late 1980s onward, the French Basque Country experienced a new form of governance based on a multi-sectional participatory approach combining state, local authorities, socioeconomic actors, and social movements (Chaussier 2002; Ahedo 2005). This has led to the creation of innovative territorial institutions, such as the Basque Cultural Institute in 1990, the Council for Development and the Council of the Elected Representatives of the Basque Country in 1994–1995 and the Public Office of the Basque Language in 2005. Although these institutions were initially perceived by some scholars as "cosmetic decentralization" (Mansvelt Beck 2005, 37), as a form of private institutionalization in compensation for the state's refusal to create a Basque *département* (Letamendia 1997, 39), or as a depoliticization process through a more technical type of territorial planning (Ségas 2004), they nevertheless had a real policy impact. Expert work carried out by the Council for Development resulted in concrete measures such as territorial contracts in 1997, 2000, and 2008 involving the state, the regional council, the *département* authorities, and the municipalities. Although the cooperatives did not openly intervene in the creation of these bodies, leaders of the cooperative movement played a key role in this process of territorial institutionalization. Both the first president and the chief executive officer of the first Council for Development in the Basque Country were leading figures of the cooperative movement. They acted as intermediaries between public administrations, the corporate world, the social economy, and the social movements, in a context of strong, and sometimes violent, politicization of territorial identity.

They could thus acquire some legitimacy in the public sphere and shape the set of references on which the new territorial policies were buttressed. Worker cooperatives were also represented in the Council for Development, as part of an effort to better represent civil society in local development planning. Indeed, the Basque nationalists' local ideological supremacy over the social economy was itself challenged in the 2000s, especially by environmentalist groups and parties (Jérôme 2010). Cooperativism, once perceived here by left-wing ideologists as some form of concession to capitalism with a touch of Basque nationalism, was thus rejuvenated and seized by new territorial actors with a pluralist ideological background.

The third favorable factor was the increasing institutionalization of cross-border relations, which started in the 1990s and 2000s. European integration gave new momentum to this trend. The cooperative movement, together with other actors, seized the opportunities offered by the EU to develop new transnational partnerships. In the Basque border zone, existing networks of cultural and socio-economic activists took on a more institutional dimension (Ahedo, Etxeberria, and Letamendia 2004; Letamendia 1997). Beyond their purely commercial relations, actors in the French Basque cooperative movement took full advantage of such new opportunities to give new impetus, under a more institutionalized form, to the old cross-border partnership with the Spanish Basque cooperative networks. As a direct emanation of the cooperative movement, the association Hezkuntek,[150] founded in 2003, offers an illustration of the relation between a shared Basque identity, economic considerations, and cross-border cooperation. In line with the initial utopian tenets of the Basque cooperative movement, Hezkuntek's aim was "to further industrial development in Lapurdi, Lower Navarre, and Zuberoa through the promotion of technical and vocational training in the Basque-speaking population."[151] The main idea was to promote professional training in the Basque language, which was a way for the program initiators to show the economic functionality of minority languages and improve the image of vocational train-

---

150 Neologism, from *hezkuntza* (training), and *teknikoa* (technical).
151 Statutes of Hezkuntek.

ing. In 2003, Hezkuntek received financial support from Udalbiltza, a cross-border association of local elected representatives, and in 2006 Hezkuntek signed a convention with the Basque autonomous government to facilitate access to vocational training programs in Euskadi for French Basque students. The program was promoted by SCOPs and by various teaching institutes on the French side, and by Mondragón in Spain. Significantly, new emphasis was placed on the role of the Basque language in the resurgence of cross-border relations between French and Spanish Basque cooperatives. One of the objectives of Hezkuntek was to fight the negative image associated with the noneconomic functionality of minority languages (Keating 1998, 155; Williams 1997, 129), principally by insisting on the relevance of Basque for cross-border relations. European programs such as INTERREG also helped to reinforce cross-border links (Harguindéguy 2007) and eventually the cooperative movement itself (Itçaina and Manterola 2013).[152]. And the Basque social movement also used new European policy instruments that were specifically dedicated to both transnational cooperation and the cooperative sector. In 2009, the institutionalization of cross-border relations in which Basque-language teaching was concerned reached a new stage with the constitution of a European cooperative society associating Northern and Southern federations of Basque-language schools, the *ikastolak*. The constitution of this cooperative crowned a process begun in 1993 with the transformation of the Confederation of *Ikastolas* in the Basque Country into a European Economic Interest Grouping (EEIG). The European framework was then used to strengthen a cooperative form of organization on a territorial basis (Itçaina and Errotabehere 2018).

---

152 As a significant illustration, the ARIPTIC project, financed by INTERREG III (2000–2006), regrouped two entities, ARIZMENDI KOOP and INSUP. ARIZMENDI KOOP, a Mondragón cooperative, promotes education and training programs, in which there is an emphasis on teaching in the Basque language. INSUP, a training body in Aquitaine, has developed its activities in the field of integration programs for young people. Both bodies had already been partners in projects financed by INTERREG II or the Aquitaine-Euskadi Common Fund, which led to the creation of a European Economic Interest Grouping (ARINSUP) in 2002, the first step toward a European Cooperative Society.

Conclusion

In quantitative terms, the organizational model of the production cooperatives remained marginal in the French Basque local economy. The 524 jobs generated by the 31 French Basque SCOPs (in 2017) are indeed a remarkable achievement in the Aquitaine region. By all accounts, diffusion of the cooperative model cannot be compared to the much-quoted example of Mondragón's growth model (73,635 employees in 2016[153]). In the Spanish Basque Country, the concentration of power in a "rational democracy," priority given to a sustainable collective model, the importance of the social part required of each new member, and the integration of the cooperatives have all contributed to making Mondragón a source of inspiration rather than a business model for French Basques. Since the 1990s, the challenge facing the Mondragón cooperative members has been to reconcile their strong regional ties and cooperative values with the constraints attached to their international development (Clamp 2000; Cheney 2002). In the French Basque Country, the challenge for cooperators has, more modestly, been to promote an alternative perception of economic development through several original entrepreneurial examples. They may well be economically marginal, yet they are highly significant in terms of territorial mobilization.

While research originally centered on production systems, further investigative efforts should now aim to explain the emergence of market-linked processes and consumer behavior, two domains in which we should incorporate cultural and political approaches to the economy (DiMaggio 1994). What is left of the specificities of the Basque cooperatives in their approach to market competition? How far are consumers influenced in their choice by the cooperative and/or territorial origin of the products or services they buy and use? Do public authorities facilitate, ignore, or hamper such evolutions? The French Basque movement of worker cooperatives has long been dominated by a "production-oriented" perspective: what

---

153 Mondragón Corporacion Cooperative, *Informe annual 2016*, https://www.mondragon-corporation.com/sobre-nosotros/magnitudes-economicas/informe-anual/, consulted on December 20, 2017.

was deemed as "political" was the cooperative *process* of production, and not necessarily its outcome. In the 2000s, new forms of political consumerism emerged in Basque society as elsewhere (Soule 2012, 1717), especially with the appearance of consumer networks supporting small local farmers, notably through the alternative Basque Chamber of Agriculture (Lopepe and Rivière 2010; Itçaina 2011), the development of short food circuits (Itçaina and Gomez 2015), and the launching of the Eusko social currency in 2013 (Camino 2013). Further observation should detect whether the worker cooperative movement will join, integrate, or ignore this new politicization of consumerism. Additionally, research should also pay attention to the territorial redefinitions induced by the structuration, in the period 2009–2013, of a territorial pole of social economy (PTCE – *Pôle Territorial de Coopération Economique Sud Aquitaine* – South Aquitaine Territorial Pole of Economic Cooperation). Located in Tarnos, in the south of the Landes *département*, this pole integrates several actors from the Basque social economy, leading to new territorial alliances between regional social economy operators (Demoustier and Itçaina 2018). Lastly, the Basque case would greatly benefit from a fruitful comparison with other significant examples taken from the political economy in the new European and extra-European substate territorial mobilizations.

Bibliography

Ahedo, Igor. 2005. "Nationalism in the French Basque Country." *Regional and Federal Studies* 15, no.1: 75–91.

Ahedo, Igor, Noemi Etxeberria, and Francisco Letamendia. 2004. *Redes transfronterizas intervascas*. Bilbao: Universidad del País Vasco.

Arthur, Len, Tom Keenoy, Russell Smith, Molly Scott Cato, and Peter Anthony. 2004. "Cooperative production – a contentious space?" Paper for the 22nd Annual International Labour Process Conference, Amsterdam, April 5–7.

Azkarraga Etxegibel, Joseba. 2007. *Nor bere patroi. Arrasateko kooperatibistak aro globalaren aurrean*. Vitoria-Gasteiz: Eusko Jaurlaritza.

Azurmendi, Joxe. 1984. *El hombre cooperativo. Pensamiento de Arizmendi-arrieta.* Arantzazu: Lankide Aurrezkia, Editorial franciscana Arantzazu.

Bekemans, Léonce. 1998. "A European Model for Culture and Economic Development: Reflections and Perspectives." In *Culture and Economic Development in the Regions of Europe,* edited by Alan Kilday. Llangollen: Ectarc.

Bray, Zoe. 2006. "Basque Militant Youths in France: New Experiences of Ethnonational Identity in the European Context." *Nationalism and Ethnic Politics* 12, nos. 3–4: 533–53.

Caillé, Alain. 1990. "Présentation: La socio-économie, une nouvelle discipline?" *Revue du MAUSS* 9: 3–10.

Camino, Xabi. 2013. *L'eusko. Une monnaie complémentaire en Pays basque, outil de relocalisation de l'économie.* Bordeaux: Mémoire IFAID Aquitaine.

Cassier, Benoit, Jean-Marc Clerc, Danièle Demoustier, and Damien Rousselière. 2003. *L'entreprise collective: unité et diversité de l'économie sociale et solidaire.* Rapport de recherche DIES-MiRe. Grenoble: ESEAC IEP de Grenoble.

Chaussier, Jean-Daniel. 2002. "Le projet d'un département au Pays Basque: réalités autour d'un mythe local." In *Pays Basque un département? Une revendication citoyenne dans un cadre républicain,* edited by Claude Perrotin, Jean-Daniel Chaussier, and Eric Kerrouche. Anglet: Atlantica.

Cheney, George. 2002. *Values at Work: Employee Participation Meets Market Pressure at Mondragón.* 2nd ed. Ithaca: ILR Press; Cornell University Press.

Clamp, Christina A. 2000. "The Internationalization of Mondragón." *Annals of Public and Cooperative Economics* 71, no. 4: 557–77.

Demoustier, Danièle. 2001. *L'économie sociale et solidaire. S'associer pour entreprendre autrement.* Paris: Syros.

————, ed. 2004. Économie sociale et développement local. Les cahiers de l'économie sociale 4. Paris: Institut de l'économie sociale; L'Harmattan.

Demoustier, Danièle, and Xabier Itçaina. 2018. *Faire territoire par la coopération. L'expérience du Pôle Territorial de Coopération Economique Sud-Aquitaine.* Sarrant: La Librairie des Territoires (forthcoming).

DiMaggio, Paul. 1994. "Culture and Economy." In *The Handbook of Economic Sociology*, edited by Neil J. Smelser and Richard Swedberg. Princeton: Princeton University Press.

Faulk, Karen Ann. 2008. "If They Touch One of Us, They Touch All of Us: Cooperativism as a Counterlogic to Neoliberal Capitalism." *Anthropological Quarterly* 8, no. 3: 579–614.

Fernández de Larrinoa, Kepa. 2009. "Pastoreo en Sola. De la transhumancia a los pastos de altitud y a las queserías en el fondo del valle." *Ager. Revista de desploblación y de desarrollo rural* 8: 25–43.

Fourquet, François. 1988. *Planification et développement local au Pays Basque.* Rapport final de recherche pour le Commissariat général au Plan. Bayonne: Ikerka.

George, Donald A. R. 1997. "Self-management and Ideology." *Review of Political Economy* 9, no. 1: 51–62.

Harguindéguy, Jean-Baptiste. 2007. "Cross-border Policy in Europe. Implementing INTERREG III-A France-Spain." *Regional and Federal Studies* 17, no. 3: 317–34.

Harrisson, Denis. 2003. "Les représentations de la confiance entre gestionnaires et représentants syndicaux. Une analyse qualitative." *Relations industrielles* 58, no. 1: 109–34.

Huntzinger, France. 1994. "Forces et faiblesses du mouvement SCOP dans la crise." *Revue d'études coopératives, mutualistes et associatives* 253–254: 38–47.

Itçaina, Xabier. 2009. "La représentation agricole en débat: le cas du Pays Basque français." *Economie rurale* 312: 52–65.

―――. 2011. "Mobilisation territoriale autour d'un projet agricole en Pays Basque." In *L'Année sociale*, edited by Sophie Béroud, Nathalie Dompnier, and David Garibay. Paris: Syllepses.

Itçaina, Xabier, and Armelle Gomez. 2015. "Territorial Identity and Grassroots Economic Activism: The Politicization of Farmers' Mobilizations in the French Basque Country." *Partecipazione e Conflitto* 8, no. 2: 478–503.

Itçaina, Xabier, and Jean-Jacques Manterola. 2013. "Towards Cross-border Network Governance? The Social and Solidarity Economy and the Construction of a Cross-Border Territory in the Basque Country." In *Living on the Border: European Border Regions in Comparison*, edited by Katarzyna Stoklosa. Berlin: LIT.

Itçaina, Xabier, and Marc Errotabehere. 2018. "The Social Economy in Borderscapes: The Changing Cross-border Dynamics of Social Economy in the Basque Country." In *Social and Solidarity-based Economy and Territory: From Embeddedness to Co-construction*, edited by X. Itçaina and Nadine Richez-Battesti. CIRIEC Series on Social and Public Economy. Brussels: Peter Lang.

Jacob, James E. 1994. *Hills of Conflict: Basque Nationalism in France.* Reno: University of Nevada Press.

Jérôme, Vanessa. 2010. "L'économie sociale et solidaire, une subversion institutionnelle et politique?" In *La politique du lien. Les nouvelles dynamiques territoriales de l'économie sociale et solidaire*, edited by Xabier Itçaina. Rennes: Presses Universitaires de Rennes.

Kasmir, Sharryn. 1996. *The Myth of Mondragón: Cooperatives, Politics and Working-class Life in a Basque Town.* Albany: State University of New York Press.

Keating, Michael. 1998. *The New Regionalism in Western Europe: Territorial Restructuring and Political Change.* Northampton: Edward Elgar.

Keating, Michael, John Loughlin, and Kris Deschouwer. 2003. *Culture, Institutions and Economic Development: A Study of Eight European Regions.* Northampton: Edward Elgar.

Larralde, Xavier. 2007. "Risque stratégique et entreprise coopérative: le cas de la société de services informatiques SEI." PhD diss. Université Montesquieu Bordeaux IV.

Laville, Jean-Louis. 2000. *L'économie sociale et solidaire en Europe*. Les notes de l'Institut Karl Polanyi. Paris: CRIDA.

Letamendia, Francisco. 1997. "Basque Nationalism and Cross-border Co-operation between the Southern and Northern Basque Countries." *Regional and Federal Studies* 7, no. 2: 25–41.

Lopepe, Maritxu, and Rémi Rivière. 2010. *EHLG. Pièces à conviction*. Bayonne: Elkar.

Lougarot, Gisèle, ed. 2005. *Économie locale et identité culturelle. Retour sur image*. Anglet: Hemen.

Mansvelt Beck, Jan. 2005. *Territory and Terror: Conflicting Nationalism in the Basque Country*. Abingdon: Routledge.

Menzani, Tito. 2007. *La cooperazione in Emilia-Romana. Dalla Resistenza alla svolta degli anni settenta*. Bologna: Il Mulino.

Palard, Jacques. 2009. *La Beauce inc. Capital social et capitalisme régional*. Montréal: Presses de l'Université de Montréal.

Schneiberg, Marc, Marissa King, and Thomas Smith. 2008. "Social Movements and Organizational Form: Cooperative Alternatives to Corporations in the American Insurance, Dairy, and Grain Industries." *American Sociological Review* 73, no. 4: 635–67.

Ségas, Sébastien. 2004. "La grammaire du territoire: action publique de développement et lutte politique dans les 'pays'." PhD diss. Université de Bordeaux IV.

Smith, Andy. 2008. "Territory and the Regulation of Industry: Examples from Scotland and Aquitaine." *Regional and Federal Studies* 18, no. 1: 37–53.

Soulet, Sarah A. 2012. "Social Movements and Markets, Industries and Firms." *Organization Studies* 33, no. 12: 1715–33.

Syssner, Josefina. 2009. "Conceptualizations of Culture and Identity in Regional Politics." *Regional and Federal Studies* 19, no. 3: 437–58.

Tremlett, Giles. 2001. "Basque Co-op Protects Itself With Buffer of
    Foreign Workers." *The Guardian,* October 23, 2001.
Williams, Colin H. 1997. "Territory, Identity and Language." In *The
    Political Economy of Regionalism,* edited by Michael Keating and
    John Loughlin. London and Portland, OR: Frank Cass.

8

Denaturalization, Transformation, and Regeneration in the Social Economy: Reflections on the Mondragon Cooperative Experience in the Age of Globalization[154]

IGNACIO BRETOS AND ANJEL ERRASTI

The viability of cooperatives in a capitalist environment has been a central theme of debate presented by Marxists since the end of the nineteenth century. Concerning discussion of the emancipatory power of cooperatives in the sphere of production, Marx argued that these organizations can constitute a force for transformation as they reflect structural possibilities within social-democratic production. Nevertheless, he also pointed to the contradictions they fall prey to, given that they must thrive and operate under a preeminently capitalist system (Marx 1967). The Marxist tradition

---

154 Activity conducted within the framework of the Research Group "Gizarte Ekonomia eta bere Zuzenbidea," GIU17/052, attached to the GEZKI Institute, University of the Basque Country (UPV/EHU).

developed this thesis employing more pessimistic terms, suggesting that cooperatives only reproduce the defects of the capitalist model (Luxemburg 1900; Mandel 1975). In a similar vein, Fabian socialists such as Sidney and Beatrice Webb (Webb and Webb 1914) held that cooperatives are not viable options for the long term, because they tend to collapse as "democracies of producers" and to shift towards being "associations of capitalists" in a process whereby worker participation diminishes substantially, power and control remain in the hands of an oligarchy, the acquisition of profits becomes a primary objective, and the worker-members' collective is gradually replaced through the hiring of nonmember employees.

These works gave rise to a later development, fundamentally during the 1970s and 1980s, in the shape of the "degeneration thesis" (see among others, Meister 1974; Ben-ner 1984; Miyazaki 1984), which suggests that cooperatives are inexorably doomed to fail in commercial terms or to degenerate into conventional forms of business activity under organizational models and priorities similar to those prevailing in the capitalist firm. However, other academic works posed an alternative to this highly determinist negative view of the cooperative life cycle, developing the "regeneration thesis" (Batstone 1983; Rosner 1984; Stryjan 1994; Cornforth 1995), which suggests that cooperatives are able to maintain their original nature in the long term, and that degeneration may be a temporary stage followed by the dynamization of regeneration processes with the power to restore the democratic, participative, social functioning of these organizations.

Over these last two decades marked by the intensification of the neoliberal globalization process, a renewed debate has emerged around the viability of cooperatives and their ability to retain their cooperative practices and values while maintaining their competitiveness in the capitalist market (Atzeni 2012; Bretos and Marcuello 2017). As John Storey Imanol Basterretxea, and Graeme Salaman (2014) point out, degeneration has, historically, been the prism that has dominated the analysis of cooperatives and continues to display signs of scientific hegemony (see also Cornforth 1995 for a lengthy critique of the literature on cooperative degeneration). In this regard, several works have focused on degenerative trends experienced, in democratic and participative terms, by cooperatives operating in highly dynamic markets (Cathcart 2013, 2014; Paranque and Willmott 2014). In contrast, other works have concentrated on the possibilities cooperatives offer for reinvigorating worker participation in the firm and standing up to oligarchic management pressures that can arise within these organizations (Hernandez 2006; Ng and Ng 2009; Storey, Basterretxea, and Salaman 2014; Jaumier 2017; Narvaiza et al. 2017). It must be said, though, that these studies have generally been limited to the analysis of small and medium-sized cooperatives that exclusively unfold their activity at the domestic level.

In consequence, while this literature has provided essential contributions, our knowledge of the degenerative and regenerative dynamics that occur in big multinational cooperatives is extremely limited. This research is essential when we consider that cooperatives are being compelled to develop internationalization strategies in pursuit of survival in increasingly competitive globalized sectors (McMurtry and Reed 2009; Bretos and Marcuello 2017). The well-known Mondragon cooperative group provides a fruitful terrain for study of these issues, insomuch as many of its industrial cooperatives are organized as multinational enterprises. To be specific, our work explores, on one hand, the degenerative tendencies experienced by Mondragon's multinational cooperatives through a deterioration in worker participation in favor of greater managerial control, the redefinition of cooperative values in accordance with economic efficiency and productivity, and the setting-up of capitalist subsidiaries in which the workers are simply wage-earners. Meanwhile, we examine the regeneration strategies promoted in these multinational cooperatives, placing particular emphasis on the regenerative initiatives designed to export the cooperative model to capitalist subsidiaries.

For these purposes, this study rests on recent empirical works concerning the Mondragon group, along with the authors' own qualitative research conducted over the last few years in some of the most important multinational cooperatives in the group: Fagor Ederlan, Maier, and Fagor Electrodomesticos. This qualitative research utilizes primary and secondary data. The primary data comes from the holding of a great number of in-depth interviews with senior managers in Mondragon and different organizational actors both from the parent cooperatives and from domestic and foreign subsidiaries (taking in managers, expatriates, rank-and-file worker-members, union representatives, employees on temporary contracts, and representatives of the cooperatives' governing bodies). The secondary data, meanwhile, was obtained from a variety of internal records provided by Mondragon and the cooperatives (annual reports, sustainability and social responsibility reports, strategic plans, social statutes, and so on) and from information publicly available in press releases, corporate magazines, audiovisual documents, and similar material.

Following this introduction, the next section shows a contemporary "snapshot" of the Mondragon group. The third section analyzes the different degenerative tendencies experienced by Mondragon's multinational cooperatives, while the fourth explores the most significant regeneration strategies that have been launched. Lastly, the final section gathers together the principal conclusions of the study and draws out some essential implications for the development of organizational theory in relation to cooperatives.

The Mondragon Cooperative System: A General View

A key aspect that the regional system of governance in the Basque Country is built on is "associationalism" (Cooke, Uranga, and Etxebarria 1997), rooted in a long tradition of working-class activism, organizational democracy, and participation in the areas of work and the community (Caro Baroja 1974). Today, this historical model is reflected in the marked presence of worker-owned firms in the Basque region (Bretos and Morandeira 2016). The *Mondragon Cooperative Experience*, which took off more than half a century ago in the Basque Country, is probably the best representation of this institutional environment (Whyte and Whyte 1991; Kasmir 1996; Cheney 2002). Since its origins, it was an experience anchored in the needs of the local environment, with the creation in 1943 of what is today the University of Mondragon, of the industrial cooperative Ulgor (later to be called Fagor Electrodomesticos) in 1956, and the cooperative credit entity Laboral Kutxa and the system of social protection Lagun Aro in 1959. These four branches clinched the development of the community, promoted hundreds of cooperatives, and consolidated what is today known as the Mondragon Corporation (Mondragon 2015). Inspired by the Catholic social doctrine of Father Jose Maria Arizmendiarrieta, these cooperatives began as small democratic organizations, with deep roots in the territory and a powerful sense of community, around the concept of *human community work*, grounded in the notion that all the workers were members and co-owners of the company (Molina and Miguez 2008).

However, the Mondragon Cooperative Experience has undergone an extraordinary transformation in recent decades. The competitive and economic pressures of globalization have forced many of its industrial cooperatives to pursue an intense growth strategy, first within the domestic market and, since the beginning of the 1990s, in international markets too. Today, the Mondragon Corporation is the first business group in the Basque Country and tenth in Spanish company ranking. The group is set up as a federation and employs 74,335 people in 261 organizations (101 of which are cooperatives) distributed over the areas of industry, finance, knowledge, and distribution. The industrial heart of Mondragon is composed of several multinational cooperatives that control roughly 130 plants abroad. These subsidiaries employ 11,796 people, representing around 40 percent of the total of employees in Mondragon's industrial division. More than 70 percent of sales correspond to international turnover (Mondragon 2016).

This transformation has its reflection in the reshaping of the Mondragon Cooperative Experience under the concept of *humanity at work*, whose new mission combines the central objectives of a business organization competing in international markets with the use of democratic methods in its company organization, the creation of employment, the human and professional promotion of its workers, and a commitment to development within its social environment (Mondragon 2015, 21). Nevertheless, cooperative values and practices continue to guide the functioning of Mondragon's parent cooperatives in the Basque Country. As owners, worker members participate in the distribution of profits and are involved in decision-making in several ways. Thus, they take part in the general assembly under the "one person/one vote" rule and can be elected as members of the governing council and of the social council (Cheney 2005). The governance structure of a Mondragon cooperative is represented in Figure 2.

Figure 8.2:
Governance structure of a first-tier cooperative

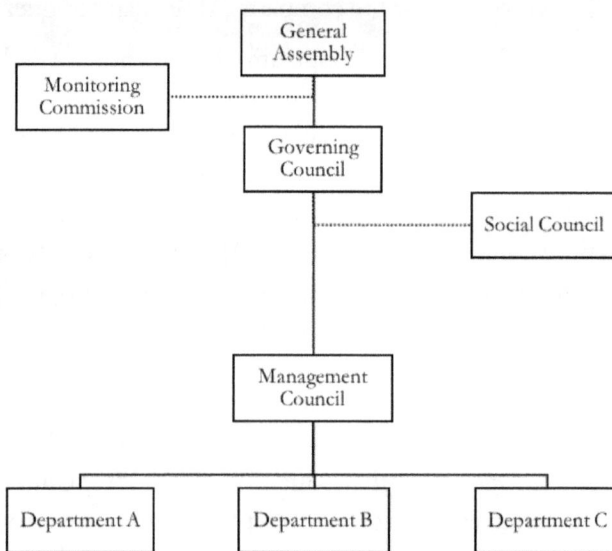

Source: adapted from Altuna, Loyola, and Pagalday (2013) and Whyte and Whyte (1991)

The general assembly is the cooperative's supreme body and expresses the corporate will as manifested by all the members. It comprises all the cooperative members and meets at least once a year. This body approves the cooperative's strategic plans and appoints the governing council, the social council and the monitoring commission. The governing council is the organ of representation and governance, and its members are elected at the general assembly. This body is responsible for governing and representing the company, and its decisions are subordinated to the policies and strategies set by the general assembly. It supervises the administration, appoints the manager, and monitors his or her performance. The purpose of the monitoring commission is to decide on the proper implementation of accounting aspects and other issues that require its attention. The social council fulfils a role resembling that of a union. It is a consultative body that represents the members in the cooperative's internal proceedings. It has an advisory function of social communication and acts as a channel between management and workers. The members are chosen by work areas and are ratified by the general assembly. Its functions involve employment counseling, information, negotiation, and social control. Lastly, the management council is the executive body that manages the cooperative. It is formed by the board members and the manager, who is appointed by the governing council and can be removed from office by worker-members (Altuna, Loyola, and Pagalday 2013; Whyte and Whyte, 1991).

Meanwhile, in the work area, workers participate by means of different mechanisms, including joint meetings between workers and management. Internal promotion and job stability are, likewise, paramount for Mondragon (Heras 2014). The dismissal of members is extremely unusual and, in the event of the occasional closure of a plant, its members are relocated within other cooperatives in the group. In a similar vein, the wage differentials in the group's cooperatives are strikingly low, although they have increased from the original scale of 1:3 to today's 1:8 in some cases. As a last point, it should be noted that members receive training both in technical and business aspects, and in the culture and values of the Mondragon Cooperative Experience (Basterretxea and Albizu 2011).

Multinational Transformation and Degenerative Pressures

Although the Mondragon cooperatives have, since their origin, been subject to contradictory demands between democratic institutional logics and those of the capitalist market, the changes brought about by increasing globalization and competition in markets since the 1980s have intensified these tensions (Taylor 1994). Internationalization is a clear consequence. Some industrial cooperatives have been compelled to grow at an international level since the early 1990s to remain competitive and safeguard the jobs of worker members in the Basque plants.

In various ways internationalization and global competition have influenced the transformation of the original values and practices of these cooperatives (see also Bretos and Errasti 2017; Bretos, Errasti, and Marcuello 2018). Our research identified several dynamics that fundamentally affect governance and the nature and scope of worker participation in cooperatives. In first place, the greater organizational size of cooperatives, and the greater complexity of the strategic decisions that must be taken due to being immersed in business dynamics that are changing and global, have been key factors that have affected people's participation. When interviewed, several members recognized a certain ritualization of the general assemblies and other democratic spaces, remarking that they had become symbolic spaces rather than structures in which people really participated.

Similarly, the intensification of the requirements of economic efficiency, stemming from global competition and international growth, has meant that self-management and participation have been displaced in favor of oligarchic management tendencies (Heras 2014). This transformation has been driven by the greater power of control bestowed on managers who are often more committed to efficiency than to the cooperative culture, coupled with a managerial discourse focused on competitiveness that privileges the interests of profitability and growth (Taylor 1994; Heras and Basterretxea 2016).

These factors are reflected by the fact that Mondragon's multinational cooperatives have imported prevailing models of total quality management, lean production, and just-in-time inventory systems (Cheney 2005; Heras 2014). Many cooperatives in the early 2000s, for instance, introduced the "mini-company" system aimed at encouraging efficiency and productivity through stronger worker motivation. Mini-companies, in short, constitute a way of structuring the organization so that each of its units runs as a small autonomous firm in which the workers take decisions and resolve problems connected with the work area in the same space in which they occur. As was observed in our research, these management models have inculcated a weak, superfluous culture of self-management that promotes forms of managerially controlled participation, limited to low levels of decision-making in the work area, and assessed in terms of employee motivation and commitment to managerial objectives established from above (see also Cheney 2002; Heras 2014; Bretos and Errasti 2017; Bretos, Errasti, and Marcuello 2018).

Meanwhile, the very model of internationalization pursued by the Mondragon cooperatives constitutes a contradiction. On one hand, the internationalization strategy has been grounded in a "multi-location" strategy (Luzarraga 2008), that is to say, an expansionist strategy given that new activity opened up abroad does not imply the closure of any preexisting activity within the domestic market. On the other hand, both domestic and international growth has nevertheless been based on the setting-up of non-cooperative subsidiaries (capitalist companies) in which the workers are simply employees and, in consequence, do not enjoy the same rights as cooperative members in the parent companies, since they do not share in the ownership, distribution of profits, and management of their enterprises (Bretos and Errasti 2017; Bretos, Errasti, and Marcuello 2018). Indeed, although the parent cooperatives have kept up a high proportion of cooperative members as compared with nonmember employees (the member collective makes up around 80 percent of those employed), if jobs in the subsidiaries are also included, this proportion falls to

30 percent. In this regard, between 1991 and 2007, the percentage of cooperative employment in the whole Mondragon group dropped from 86 percent to 29.5 percent (Storey, Basterretxea, and Salaman 2014).

In general terms, multi-location has provided the Mondragon cooperatives with extraordinary results, favoring job creation both in the Basque Country and abroad, and endowing them with flexibility to face the economic recession in better conditions (Elortza, Alzola, and Lopez 2012; Luzarraga and Irizar 2012). The number of those employed in the Fagor Ederlan Group, for example, rose from 1,300 workers in 1999 to 3,700 in 2015. By contrast, this pattern was not so evident with the crash of Fagor Electrodomesticos, a symbolic circumstance of great economic and social impact, the company having been the flagship of the Mondragon group. Multi-location afforded Fagor impressive results for years. However, while in 2007 the group employed 11,000 workers, before its collapse in 2013 only 5,500 remained in the group (1,900 of them in the Basque Country). The crash undergone by this cooperative was, in fact, fundamentally due to market conditions, although that does not make it exempt from a range of problems associated with governance, such as those referred to above (Errasti, Bretos, and Etxezarreta 2016; Errasti, Bretos, and Nunez 2017).

The internal mechanisms of the Mondragon system have been crucial for coping with this scenario. Today, the overwhelming majority of the cooperative members affected by the closure of Fagor in the Basque Country have encountered a solution, mainly through relocation in other cooperatives in the group. Thousands of nonmember employees in the cooperative and its subsidiaries, however, have been excluded from Mondragon's solidarity mechanisms. That throws the contradictions of these multinational cooperatives into sharp relief, not only where democratic and participatory deficiencies in the capitalist subsidiaries are concerned, but also in terms of the social and working conditions offered in these subsidiaries (Kasmir 2016).

Dynamics of Regeneration in Mondragon's Multi-national Cooperatives

After decades of growth that have distanced some Mondragon cooperatives from their social cooperative nature in favor of managerial prerogatives and a market orientation, the group has been enveloped, since the mid-2000s, in a process of reflection directed at refreshing essential aspects of the cooperative model, including social and community transformation, worker participation, democratic governance, intercooperation, and cooperative training and education (Azkarraga, Cheney, and Udaondo 2012). This reflection has resulted in the implementation of regeneration strategies in several cooperatives in the group. On a general level, regeneration initiatives exist to reinvigorate the original practices and values in the parent cooperatives, on one hand, and to extend the cooperative model to the capitalist subsidiaries, on the other.

Revitalization of Cooperative Values and Practices in the Basque Parent Cooperatives

Various large multinational industrial cooperatives in the Mondragon group have been attempting, particularly since 2005, to promote projects to recover and revitalize the original cooperative values and practices (Azkarraga, Cheney, and Udaondo 2012; Webb and Cheney 2014).

While in the 1990s education about the philosophical, social, and practical aspects of the cooperative movement took second stage to the benefit of technical training (Cheney 2002), in recent years a diversity of projects have been introduced to renovate and institutionalize cooperative training and education in Mondragon cooperatives (Webb and Cheney 2014). These projects are designed and promoted by the LANKI Institute of Cooperative Research at the University of Mondragon and by Otalora, the Mondragon management and cooperative development center. In general terms, the aim is not only to strengthen management competencies and facilitate managers' professional development, but also to attend to aspects including cultural development (focused on fostering business management in tune with a more cooperative, constructive, and organizational culture), cooperative education (addressed toward providing members of the social bodies with training so they can perform their role competently and advance a feeling of belonging to the cooperative culture and cooperative values among worker members), and social skills such as cooperative leadership and team work (Azkarraga, Cheney, and Udaondo 2012; Basterretxea and Albizu 2011).

This revitalization in cooperative education and training also acts as a support for projects being developed to boost participation both in the social bodies and in the work area. This is fundamentally happening through the reshaping and deepening of communication in the cooperatives. For years now, preparatory meetings prior to the general assemblies have been encouraged in several cooperatives, held in small groups of between thirty and forty members, the purpose being to lubricate the transmission of information and stimulate participation in those spaces. Informative talks that have traditionally been held to inform workers about key issues in the cooperative are being streamlined to spark off greater participation, dialogue, and reflection. Likewise, the social council has been a prime target for transformative and innovative initiatives. In recent years, several cooperatives have created what are known as "mini-councils," which are periodic meetings to facilitate communication between rank-and-file workers and the social council representatives. In light of the saturation affecting the social council due to its use by workers as a channel for expressing their complaints, which is a regular problem in the Mondragon cooperatives, Fagor Ederlan has set up "social plant meetings." On a monthly basis, someone from the permanent commission of the central council, the plant manager, a person from the social management team, and the social members at the plant, meet to share information about the management of the plant, settle social problems in their area, and propose subjects to pass on to the social council. Similarly, "social business councils" have also been created, bringing together someone from the governing council, the product line director, a member of the social management, and the social members participating in the business. In these spaces information to do with management is shared, general cooperative matters are discussed, and social affairs that fall outside the remit of the plant meetings are dealt with.

Other particularly dynamic and innovative industrial cooperatives, like Fagor Arrasate, are also experimenting internally with new forms of participation (Webb and Cheney 2014). This cooperative has fostered more participatory dynamics via a more qualitative treatment of information and the opening-up of spaces for deliberation and more active participation from people. One example is that the advisor's role has been redefined, not only to inform but also to energize participation in the mini-councils. The latter have, in turn, been reshaped to encourage the advisory role of the social council.

Extension of the Cooperative Model to the Capitalist Subsidiaries

Beyond these aspects, which fundamentally affect the revitalization of participation and democratic governance in the Basque parent cooperatives, a particularly significant novel feature consists of the passing, in 2003, of the "social expansion strategy" by Mondragon's cooperative congress. This strategy is a matter of the propagation of cooperative values throughout the capitalist subsidiaries via the development of participation mechanisms for workers, resembling those prevailing in the cooperatives (Irizar 2005). This congress agreed on crucial objectives: namely, to encourage greater transparency in decision-making in the subsidiaries, implement the same participative management model applied in the cooperatives, advance toward having at least 30 percent of ownership in the workers' hands, and devoting between 1 percent and 5 percent of profits to local development in the territories in which the subsidiaries are located (Flecha and Ngai 2014). Later, the corporate management model[155] included

---

155 The corporate management model is the general tool created to homogenize management of all the cooperatives in the Mondragon group and its subsidiaries. This model is not a detailed action plan, nor does it involve

three essential aspects to be given priority in the cooperatives: Self-management, communication, and corporate development (Mondragon 2013). The first two (self-management and communication) encompass both the cooperatives and their subsidiaries, while the third category (corporate development) is designed fundamentally for the subsidiaries. Where self-management in cooperatives and subsidiaries is concerned, the corporation stresses the design of horizontal organizational structures to facilitate participation and team work and enable the collective definition of aims and taking responsibility. Communication is focused on establishing policies of transparency to stimulate interpersonal relations and information flow in the entire organization. Lastly, corporate development concentrates on exporting the cooperative model to the capitalist firms by means of the introduction of the cooperative management model.

In recent years, these general guidelines, although they do not constitute rules that must be obligatorily complied with, have resulted in a variety of concrete actions taken by some multinational cooperatives, designed to promote the "cooperativization" of subsidiaries, through implementation of the cooperative model in them. Two main lines of cooperativization can be distinguished in Mondragon. The first and most direct involves the outright transformation of capitalist subsidiaries into cooperatives, and has been used exclusively in the case of domestic subsidiaries. The second line of action, devised in the main for foreign subsidiaries, is based on the partial implementation of some management practices associated with the cooperative model that characterizes the Basque parent companies.

---

obligatory compliance on the part of the group's cooperatives; rather, it provides general guidelines that each cooperative adapts to its particular context, these being addressed to achieve business management that is both efficient and consistent with Mondragon's corporate culture (Mondragon 2013).

Cooperativization of Domestic Subsidiaries

The cooperativization of the domestic subsidiaries has mainly been carried out by means of two formulas. One involves the creation of a mixed cooperative,[156] in that the subsidiary becomes a cooperative whose ownership is normally distributed between the actual subsidiary workers, the parent company, and Mondragon Inversiones S. Coop. The other means that, although the subsidiary keeps its legal status, the workers become members of the parent cooperative in the shape of seconded members,[157] thereby gaining access to the ownership, profits, and management of the firm. Some of the first experiences developed by multinational cooperatives came about at Fagor Electrodomesticos. In the late 1990s, the Basque subsidiary Fabrelec S.A. became a cooperative (later to be called Edesa S. Coop.), ownership of which was distributed among the subsidiary's worker members, with a 44 percent share, and the parent Fagor Electrodomesticos. In 2004, the 250 workers of the Basque subsidiary Geyser Gastech became seconded members of the parent cooperative (Errasti and Mendizabal 2007).

In recent years, particularly noteworthy experiences have taken place in this area (for detailed analyses of the cooperativization of domestic subsidiaries in Mondragon, see Flecha and Ngai 2014; Bretos and Errasti 2016, 2017), in which the cases of Maier and Fagor Ederlan stand out. In 2006, most of the 80 workers at the Basque subsidiary Fit Automoción S.A. became seconded members of the parent company Fagor Ederlan; a similar process to that which was recently completed at its other Basque subsidiary Victorio Luzuriaga Usurbil. Meanwhile, in 2008, Victorio Luzuriaga Tafalla S.A., a subsidiary of Fagor Ederlan based in Navarre, was

---

156 A mixed cooperative differs from a conventional cooperative, fundamentally in the structure of corporate governance. As defined by Basque cooperative law, mixed cooperatives have minority shareholders, whose voting rights in the general assembly can be determined, exclusively or preferentially, in accordance with their capital contributions.

157 Seconded members are those who maintain a company link with the cooperative and offer their services in an organization that the cooperative cooperates with or participates in.

transformed into the mixed cooperative Fagor Ederlan Tafalla S. Coop., and just over half of its 700 workers then took on the status of cooperative members. In 2012, the cooperative Maier conducted a similar process at its Galician subsidiary Maier Ferroplast, in which 150 of the 190 workers on the payroll endorsed the transformation of the plant into a mixed cooperative. Our research on these subsidiaries identified several positive effects stemming from their cooperativization, including greater company resilience in the years of economic crisis, improvements in job stability and relations between workers and management, greater worker participation in the firm, an ensuing increase in their motivation and commitment, and an improvement in working conditions.

Nonetheless, important limitations on these processes also exist, hampering the genuine implementation of cooperative practices and culture even despite the legal transformation of these companies into cooperatives. One fundamental limitation is the restricted access of new members to ownership of the subsidiaries. In Fagor Ederlan Tafalla, for instance, the workers acquired only 12 percent of the company, while the rest remained in the hands of the parent Fagor Ederlan and of Mondragon, which form a majority in the governance bodies of the cooperative subsidiary. In the case of Maier Ferroplast, the fact that the subsidiary was small allowed the workers to acquire a 33 percent stake. These situations result in some dissatisfaction among workers with the nature and reach of their participation in the company. An internal survey held by Fagor Ederlan Tafalla a year after cooperativization of the subsidiary revealed that 23 percent of the workers in the subsidiary gave a score of 1 out of 10 for their participation in the company. Then again, there is an evident lack of commitment and knowledge among the new members where cooperative culture and values are concerned. One year after cooperativization, only 7 percent of the workers at Fagor Ederlan Tafalla stated that they knew the content and meaning of the principles and values of the Mondragon Cooperative experience, admitting that most of them became members due to the greater job stability that the cooperative formula offered. Likewise, nonmember workers who were kept on the payroll after the cooperativization processes were excluded from the subsidiaries' democratic participative spaces (Bretos and Errasti 2016, 2017).

Cooperativization of Foreign Subsidiaries

As we indicated above, the cooperativization of the foreign subsidiaries has been based on the partial implementation of certain management practices associated with the cooperative model. Some works that have analyzed such initiatives point out that Mondragon's multinational cooperatives managed to conserve cooperative values and practices during the international expansion and to spread the cooperative model to the foreign subsidiaries (Luzarraga 2008; Lertxundi 2011; Luzarraga and Irizar 2012; Flecha and Ngai 2014; Santos-Pitanga 2015). The argument put forward by these authors is grounded fundamentally in the introduction of specific practices in the subsidiaries such as organization in self-managed teams, workers being trained in technical aspects, and greater communication between employees and management.

Our research into various foreign subsidiaries of the Mondragon group, however, yielded markedly different results (Errasti 2015; Errasti et al. 2016; Bretos and Errasti 2017; Bretos, Errasti, and Marcuello 2018). In general terms, Mondragon's multinational cooperatives have introduced three kinds of practices in a similar way in all the foreign subsidiaries. In first place, all the foreign subsidiaries operate under the same total quality management model and techniques of lean production, meaning that work organization practices in these subsidiaries substantially resemble those which prevail in the Basque cooperative workshops. In second place, the Mondragon cooperatives have implemented mechanisms of direct worker participation. Accordingly, all the subsidiaries have introduced the mini-company model, some sort of employee suggestions system, and the setting-up of periodic meetings between management and workers that encourage the exchange of information regarding productive aspects. Worker participation in the work area is therefore significant in the foreign subsidiaries. Third, all the foreign subsidiaries have brought in variable remuneration systems.

In the case of the managers, incentives are set in line with periodically established objectives, while rewards for the plant workers are linked to productivity and production quality.

Meanwhile, where other management practices associated with the cooperative model are concerned (pay equity, job stability, internal promotion, and the continuous training of workers), substantial differences are observed between subsidiaries located in different countries. It is clear, for instance, that scarcely a trace of the cooperative model remains in the Chinese subsidiaries (Errasti 2015; Bretos, Errasti, and Marcuello 2018). Other subsidiaries, in contrast, have managed to advance in the introduction of these kinds of practices to some extent. The Brazilian subsidiary of Fagor Ederlan is an example. This subsidiary has established a social balance sheet using indicators of economic, social, and environmental performance that facilitate a comparison of the characteristics of the parent company with those of the subsidiary. Among other aspects, there has been a reduction of differences in the company's wage scales; opportunities for training and internal promotion for workers have been promoted; working conditions are reexamined annually in collaboration with the unions to keep them at levels resembling or higher than those on offer in the local environment; and social benefits have been added for the workers that include, among other things, health insurance, food vouchers, and transport to the plant. All these measures have fostered workers' job stability and welfare (Bretos and Errasti 2017; Bretos, Errasti, and Marcuello 2018). In like manner, before the economic crisis struck, Fagor Electrodomesticos achieved similar advances at its plant located in Poland (Errasti et al. 2016).

Nevertheless, although the cooperative model has been more firmly consolidated in some subsidiaries, it is clear that none of them has been transformed into a cooperative or has consistently introduced the set of practices associated with the cooperative model, particularly where worker participation in the ownership, distribution of profits, and general management of the company is concerned; and these are central aspects of the cooperative formula. Our research identified various factors that stand in the way of the genuine cooperativization of the foreign subsidiaries. On the one hand, there are cultural and institutional barriers. In various countries in which the Mondragon cooperatives are located there is no legislation to legally cover the work cooperative formula, as is the case of China, for example. Evidently, that hinders the possible transformation of these subsidiaries into cooperatives. Further, many of these countries have no cooperative tradition comparable to that which exists in the Basque Country, and the employees of these subsidiaries are not accustomed to working within a work culture of cooperation. That certainly makes it hard to establish in these subsidiaries management practices rooted in participation and collective decision-making.

On the other hand, although these institutional factors are important, our research identified other obstacles, linked with parent-subsidiary power relations and with the actual interests of the parent, which seem to yet more critically impede cooperativization of the foreign subsidiaries. A key aspect is the perception held among Basque cooperative members that workers in the foreign plants do not develop such a solid commitment to the company and to the cooperative as they do, which, at the end of the day, sparks off suspicions about the success of a hypothetical project of cooperativization in a foreign plant. Likewise, managers and worker members in the parent cooperatives consider that the greater participation and autonomy of the workers in the foreign subsidiaries might prove detrimental for control by the parent over the entire business group, perceiving in consequence that the cooperativization of foreign plants might place at risk the very viability of the cooperative and the jobs of Basque cooperative members.

Conclusion

Some recent works have challenged the determinist monolithic view expressed by the "degeneration thesis," demonstrating that cooperatives are capable of coping with isomorphic institutional pressures—which drive these organizations to adopt organizational forms and priorities resembling those of a capitalist company—and of developing regeneration strategies (Ng and Ng 2009; Storey, Basterretxea, and Salaman 2014; Narvaiza et al. 2017; Jaumier 2017). This study complements these contributions on cooperative regeneration through its analysis of the degenerative and regenerative dynamics that occur in multinational cooperatives, a field in which our knowledge is still extremely limited.

As evidenced by our research, historically speaking, cooperatives and other organizations in the social economy have been exposed to degenerative pressures. Global capitalism and the transformation of some Mondragon cooperatives into multinational organizations have only accentuated already existing tensions between cooperative principles and business success within a capitalist environment, thus affecting democratic governance and participatory systems in these large market-oriented cooperatives. These tensions are fueled by various dynamics, such as the predominance of managerial control at the expense of worker participation, the reshaping of cooperative values and practices in line with the managerial priorities of efficiency and competitiveness, and the annexation of capitalist subsidiaries in which rights and benefits associated with the cooperative model, such as job stability and participation in cooperative decisions, are restricted for workers.

Nonetheless, our study also evinces that multinational cooperatives are able to design and implement various regeneration strategies geared to revitalize cooperative values and practices, through the recovery and institutionalization of cooperative education, for example, or by deepening rank-and-file worker participation and the dynamization of different democratic spaces to encourage everyone in the organization to become involved and communicate. Beyond these issues, which fundamentally concern the parent cooperatives, this work has particularly focused on cooperativization initiatives developed in recent years in the capitalist subsidiaries, both domestic and international, whose aim is to extend the cooperative model within them. While these cooperativization initiatives are not without their challenges and limitations, their transformative potential is evident. These kinds of regeneration strategies will, foreseeably, continue to be fundamental over the coming years, considering that cooperatives are undergoing increasing expansion internationally through the acquisition and creation of capitalist companies (Bretos and Marcuello 2017).

To sum up, this research also has important implications for the development of organizational theory regarding cooperatives. Unlike those who champion the degeneration thesis and assume that the challenges in balancing the economic and social dimensions in cooperatives will inescapably lead to their commercial or democratic failure, this study suggests that the best way to address and comprehend such tensions in cooperatives that compete in a market economy is through a "paradoxical approach" (Hernandez 2006; Ashforth and Reingen 2014). From this perspective, tensions and paradoxes are factors inherent to the survival of cooperatives. The challenge for these organizations lies, therefore, in finding a dynamic equilibrium aimed at unleashing positive organizational changes within a perennial struggle between workers' resistance and management control (Courpasson, Dany, and Clegg 2012). In our opinion, if a time comes when we no longer encounter tensions, paradoxes, and contradictions in cooperatives, the reason will be that these organizations have ceased to be alternative and have lost their transformative potential. In the meantime, cooperatives will have to survive with, through, and beyond those tensions.

Bibliography

Altuna, Larraitz, Aitzol Loyola, and Eneritz Pagalday. 2013. "Mondragón: The Dilemmas of a Mature Cooperativism." In *Cooperatives and Socialism: A View from Cuba*, edited by Camila Piñeiro-Harnecker. New York: Palgrave Macmillan.

Ashforth, Blake E., and Peter H. Reingen. 2014. "Functions of Dysfunction Managing the Dynamics of an Organizational Duality in a Natural Food Cooperative." *Administrative Science Quarterly* 59, no. 3: 474–516.

Atzeni, Maurizio, ed. 2012. *Alternative Work Organizations*. London: Palgrave Macmillan.

Azkarraga, Joseba, George Cheney, and Ainara Udaondo. 2012. "Workers Participation in a Globalized Market: Reflections on and from Mondragon." In *Alternative Work Organizations*, edited by Maurizio Atzeni. New York: Palgrave Macmillan.

Basterretxea, Imanol, and Eneka Albizu. 2011. "Management Training as a Source of Perceived Competitive Advantage: The Mondragon Cooperative Group Case." *Economic and Industrial Democracy* 32, no. 2: 199–222.

Batstone, Eric. 1983. "Organization and Orientation: A Life Cycle Model of French Cooperatives." *Economic and Industrial Democracy* 4, no. 2: 139–61.

Ben-ner, Avner. 1984. "On the Stability of the Cooperative Type of Organization." *Journal of Comparative Economics* 8, no. 3: 247–60.

Bretos, Ignacio, and Anjel Errasti. 2016. "Dinámicas de regeneración en las cooperativas multinacionales de Mondragón: la reproducción del modelo cooperativo en las filiales capitalistas." *CIRIEC-España: Revista de Economía Pública, Social y Cooperativa* 86: 5–34.

———. 2017. "Challenges and Opportunities for the Regeneration of Multinational Worker Cooperatives: Lessons from the Mondragon Corporation—A Case Study of the Fagor Ederlan Group." *Organization* 24, no. 2: 154–173.

Bretos, Ignacio, and Jon Morandeira. 2016. "La economía social ante la actual crisis económica en la Comunidad Autónoma del País Vasco." *REVESCO: Revista de Estudios Cooperativos* 122: 7–33.

Bretos, Ignacio, and Carmen Marcuello. 2017. "Revisiting Globalization Challenges and Opportunities in the Development of Cooperatives." *Annals of Public and Cooperative Economics* 88, no. 1: 47–73.

Bretos, Ignacio, Anjel Errasti, and Carmen Marcuello. 2018. "Ownership, Governance, and the Diffusion of HRM Practices in

Multinational Worker Cooperatives: Case-study Evidence from the Mondragon Group." *Human Resource Management Journal* 28, no. 1: 76–91.

Caro-Baroja, Julio. 1974. *Introducción A La Historia Social Y Económica Del Pueblo Vasco.* San Sebastián: Txertoa.

Cathcart, Abby. 2013. "Directing Democracy: Competing Interests and Contested Terrain in the John Lewis Partnership." *Journal of Industrial Relations* 55, no. 4: 601–20.

———. 2014. "Paradoxes of Participation: Non-union Workplace Partnership in John Lewis." *International Journal of Human Resource Management* 25, no. 6: 762–80.

Cheney, George. 2002. *Values at Work: Employee Participation Meets Market Pressure at Mondragon.* Ithaca, NY: Cornell University Press.

———. 2005. "Democracy at Work within the Market: Reconsidering the Potential." In *Worker Participation: Current Research and Future Trends,* edited by Vicki Smith. Amsterdam: Emerald.

Cooke, Philip, Mikel G. Uraga, and Goio Etxebarria. 1997. "Regional Innovation systems: Institutional and Organisational Dimensions." *Research Policy* 26: 475–91.

Cornforth, Chris. 1995. "Patterns of Cooperative Management: Beyond the Degeneration Thesis." *Economic and Industrial Democracy* 16, no. 4: 487–523.

Courpasson, David, Françoise Dany, and Stewart Clegg. 2012. "Resisters at Work: Generating Productive Resistance in the Workplace." *Organization Science* 23: 801–19.

Elortza, Naroa, Izaskun Alzola, and Urko López. 2012. "La Gestión de la Crisis en la Corporación Mondragón." *Ekonomiaz* 79, no. 1: 58–81.

Errasti, Anjel. 2015. "Mondragon's Chinese Subsidiaries: Coopitalist Multinationals in Practice." *Economic and Industrial Democracy* 36, no. 3: 479–99.

Errasti, Anjel, and Antxon Mendizabal. 2007. "The Impact of Global-
    ization and Relocation Strategies in Large Co-operatives: The
    Case of the Mondragon Co-operative Fagor Electrodomésti-
    cos S.Coop." *Advances in the Economic Analysis of Participatory and
    Labor-managed Firms* 10: 265–87.

Errasti, Anjel, Ignacio Bretos, and Enekoitz Etxezarreta. 2016. "What
    do Mondragon Coopitalist Multinationals Look Like? The
    Rise and Fall of Fagor Electrodomésticos S. Coop. and its
    European Subsidiaries." *Annals of Public and Cooperative Econom-
    ics* 87: 433–56.

Errasti, Anjel, Ignacio Bretos, and Aitziber Nunez. 2017. "The Viabil-
    ity of Cooperatives: The Fall of the Mondragon Cooperative
    Fagor." *Review of Radical Political Economics* 49, no. 2: 181–97.

Flecha, Ramón, and Pun Ngai. 2014. "The Challenge for Mondragon:
    Searching for the Co-operative Values in Times of Interna-
    tionalization." *Organization* 21, no. 5: 666–82.

Heras, Iñaki. 2014. "The Ties that Bind? Exploring the Basic Princi-
    ples of Worker-Owned Organizations in Practice." *Organization*
    21, no. 5: 645–65.

Heras, Iñaki, and Imanol Basterretxea. 2016. "Do Co-ops Speak the
    Managerial Lingua Franca? An Analysis of the Managerial
    Discourse of Mondragon Cooperatives." *Journal of Co-operative
    Organization and Management* 4, no. 1: 13–21.

Hernandez, Sarah. 2006. "Striving for Control: Democracy and
    Oligarchy at a Mexican Cooperative." *Economic and Industrial
    Democracy* 27, no. 1: 105–35.

Irizar, Inazio. 2005. *Empresa Cooperativa y Liderazgo*. Oñati: Mondragon
    Unibertsitatea.

Jaumier, Stéphane. 2017. "Preventing Chiefs from Being Chiefs: An
    Ethnography of a Co-operative Sheet-metal Factory. *Organiza-
    tion* 24, no. 2: 218–39.

Kasmir, Sharryn. 1996. *The Myth of Mondragon: Cooperatives, Politics and
    Working-Class Life in a Basque Town*. New York: SUNY Press.

————. 2016. "The Mondragon Cooperatives and Global Capitalism: A Critical Analysis." *New Labor Forum* 25, no. 1: 52–59.

Lertxundi, Aitziber. 2011. "Characteristics of Human Resource Management in Basque Cooperatives and their Response to New International Contexts." In *Basque Cooperativism*, edited by Baleren Bakaikoa and Eneka Albizu. Reno: Center for Basque Studies, University of Nevada, Reno.

Luxemburg, Rosa. 1900. *Reform or Revolution*. London: Militant Publications.

Mandel, Ernest. 1975. "Self-Management Dangers and Possibilities." *International* 2, no. 4: 3–9.

Luzarraga, Jose M. 2008. "Mondragon Multi-Localisation Strategy: Innovating a Human Centred Globalisation." PhD diss. Mondragon University.

Luzarraga, Jose M., and Iñazio Irizar. 2012. "La Estrategia de Multilocalización Internacional de la Corporación Mondragón." *Ekonomiaz* 79: 114–45.

Marx, Karl. 1967. *Capital: A Critique of Political Economy*. Vol. 1. New York: International Publishers.

McMurtry, John J., and Darryl Reed. 2009. *Co-operatives in a Global Economy*. Newcastle: Cambridge Scholars Publishing.

Meister, Albert. 1974. *La participation dans les associations*. Paris: Editions Ouvrières.

Miyazaki, Hajime. 1984. "On Success and Dissolution of the Labour-Managed Firm in the Capitalist Economy." *Journal of Political Economy* 92, no. 5: 909–31.

Molina, Fernando, and Antonio Miguez. 2008. "The Origins of Mondragon: Catholic Co-operativism and Social Movement in a Basque valley (1941–59)." *Social History* 33, no. 3: 284–98.

Mondragon. 2013. *Corporate Management Model*. Mondragón: Mondragon Corporation.

————. 2015. *A Review of the Key Milestones in the Co-operative Group's History*. Eskoriatza: Mondragon Corporation.

————. 2016. *2015 Annual Report.* Eskoriatza: Mondragon Corporation.

Narvaiza, Lorea, Cristina Aragon-Amonarriz, Cristina Iturrioz-Landart, Julie Bayle-Cordier, and Sandrine Stervinou. 2017. "Cooperative Dynamics during the Financial Crisis: Evidence from Basque and Breton Case Studies." *Nonprofit and Voluntary Sector Quarterly* 46, no. 3: 505–24.

Ng, Catherine W., and Evelyn Ng. 2009. "Balancing the Democracy Dilemmas: Experiences of Three Women Workers' Cooperatives in Hong Kong." *Economic and Industrial Democracy* 30, no. 2: 182–206.

Paranque, Bernard, and Hugh Willmott. 2014. "Cooperatives—Saviours or Gravediggers of Capitalism? Critical Performativity and the John Lewis Partnership." *Organization* 21, no. 5: 604–25.

Rosner, Menachem. 1984. "A Search for 'Coping Strategies' or Forecasts of Cooperative Degeneration?" *Economic and Industrial Democracy* 5, no. 3: 391–99.

Santos-Pitanga, Tatiana. 2015. "La institucionalización de la solidaridad: El caso Mondragón." PhD diss. University of Barcelona.

Storey, John, Imanol Basterretxea, and Graeme Salaman. 2014. "Managing and Resisting 'Degeneration' in Employee-owned Businesses: A Comparative Study of Two Large Retailers in Spain and the United Kingdom." *Organization* 21, no. 5: 626–44.

Stryjan, Yohanan. 1994. "Understanding Cooperatives: The Reproduction Perspective." *Annals of Public and Cooperative Economics* 65, no. 1: 59–80.

Taylor, Peter L. 1994. "The Rhetorical Construction of Efficiency: Restructuring and Industrial Democracy in Mondragon, Spain." *Sociological Forum* 9, no. 3: 459–89.

Webb, Tom, and George Cheney. 2014. "Worker-owned-and-governed Co-operatives and the Wider Co-operative Movement." In *The Routledge Companion to Alternative Organization,* edited by Martin

Parker, George Cheney, Valérie Fournier, and Chris Land. London: Routledge.

Webb, Sidney, and Beatrice Webb. 1921. *The Consumers' Co-operative Movement.* London: Longmans.

Whyte, William F., and Kathleen K. Whyte. 1991. *Making Mondragon: The Growth and Dynamics of the Worker Cooperative Complex.* Ithaca, NY: ILR Press.

9

Tenant Cooperatives and New Public Housing Policies in Euskadi[158]

AITZIBER ETXEZARRETA, SANTIAGO MERINO, GALA CANO, AND ARTITZAR ERAUSKIN

Very recently, the first case of active promotion of the tenant housing cooperative formula by the Basque government was announced. This would be developed on a plot of land acquired for that purpose in Donostia. Will tenant cooperatives, through this and other similar actions, acquire the rank of a public housing policy?

This chapter presents a study of the routes taken by housing cooperatives, starting with their most traditional role as an instrument for the construction of social housing (known in Spain as VPOs, Vivienda de Protección Oficial), then as a different formula for housing tenure, and now offering a new perspective in the form of tenant cooperatives as a driving force for public policies in Euskadi (the Autonomous Community of the Basque Country). Thus, the first section presents a review of the historical development of housing cooperatives from the social economy perspective (from traditional

---

158 Activity conducted within the framework of the Research Group "Gizarte Ekonomia eta bere Zuzenbidea," GIU17/052, attached to the GEZKI Institute, University of the Basque Country (UPV/EHU).

housing cooperatives to tenant cooperatives). A brief explanation is given in the second section of the results of research conducted recently around emerging initiatives involving tenant cooperatives in Spain. The third section offers an analysis of the ground traveled by institutional initiatives connected with tenant cooperatives and public housing policies in Euskadi. Lastly, the main conclusions and reflections obtained are set out.

The Social Economy and Housing: Traditional Housing Cooperatives

Housing cooperatives have been a very familiar actor in the promotion and construction of Spanish housing, because in the past they played that role to offer lower-cost housing to their members, usually as a form of ownership. The cooperative, then, once the construction period was completed, allocated the dwellings and disappeared. In recent years another phenomenon of "cooperativism" has crept into cooperative housing, under the aegis of the old development companies; following the drop in the activity and profitability of promotion and construction work, they make instrumental use of this legal formula at a far remove from what we might understand as cooperativism. This development has led to deep reflection among the different public administrations regarding this formula and the agents participating in the model (Otxoa-Errarte 2016).[159]

In our geographical setting, the tendency was for housing cooperatives to be built (as was subsidized housing) for the most disadvantaged social sectors that are liable to be excluded from the housing market, especially at moments when the housing demand situation did not encourage traditional developers to offer a limited product price (Etxezarreta and Merino 2013).

The types of housing cooperatives that have customarily been implemented most in the Spanish context have been linked to the

---

159 These "cover" cooperatives have come into being with no members and they obtain them due to publicity that underlines their advantages, but conceals the risks. This whole matter is posing many dilemmas for the courts and arbitration services.

development and construction of cooperative social housing, for subsequent assignment among the cooperative members prior to the winding up of the cooperative. The future beneficiary of the dwelling (transformed into a cooperative member) is thereby saved from paying business profits to the property developer. That is why housing cooperatives have constituted an instrument in the social economy; this mechanism, applied to the volatile property market, has sought to acquire homes at more affordable prices, and enables the democratic participation of "developer" members in decision-making (Fajardo 2013).

In specific terms, housing cooperatives in Spain have traditionally developed housing under social housing legislation (cheap affordable housing laws, the Salmón Law (1935) after Federico Salmón, Minister of Labor during the Second Republic, who promoted affordable housing, and so on). In Spain, therefore, it has fundamentally been a legal form, a tool employed for the construction of social housing: up to 90 percent of the total were social dwellings in 2003 and the remaining 10 percent were secondary or free residences by decision of the cooperative members who had been awarded them (Salinas and Sanz 2003).

Tenant Cooperatives as Innovative Experiences

Under Spanish law there are various types of cooperatives related to the housing field (Etxezarreta and Merino 2013). Only tenant cooperatives, however, would meet social economy housing criteria, given that all the other housing cooperatives are purely transitory instruments for saving the cost of paying intermediaries.

Tenant cooperatives represent another formula within cooperative housing that current legislation establishes as a possibility, although to date the system of property ownership has cornered the Spanish market. In tenant cooperatives, the cooperatives maintain ownership of the dwelling, once built, in such a way that the member only has right of use, or the right of occupancy, for the enjoyment of which s/he pays a rent, a contribution, or a lease.

This model is associated with the concept of cession of use that is also connected to what is known as the Andel model; the latter has, for decades, had deep roots in the Scandinavian countries, whereas it has practically seen no implementation in Spain, outside of occasional experiences, although the regulatory framework could countenance its application. It must be remembered that in each country there are differences in the legal structure of a housing cooperative.

In the Spanish case, the horizontal cooperative has been frequent, but outside Spain, a housing cooperative, with different meanings in different countries, retains ownership of the property, and the residents possess shares and right of use. "Limited equity cooperatives" are North American cooperatives that also place a limit on the profits that can be obtained through the sale of shares. This system, with a limited sale, is typically Danish (*bofaellesskab*), and would be comparable in Spain with tenant cooperatives, at a limited price (Durrett 2015).

In this regard, the recent adoption in the Autonomous Community of the Basque Country of Law 3/2015, June 18, on Housing, represents a considerable qualitative step forward, as it regulates this model in a detailed fashion for its future operational application in the Basque Country (Etxebizitzako Behatokia-Observatorio Vasco de la Vivienda 2015).[160]

The Andel model originated in Denmark in 1911 and witnessed significant growth until the 1970s. This model is run democratically: members who live under the Andel scheme cannot turn their dwelling into a traditional property, although they have more rights than a conventional tenant, because this model establishes indefinite use of the accommodation (Merino 2012). This approach was was especially prominent in Sweden, Denmark, and Germany. Hous-

---

160 There are also various initiatives in Catalonia in this regard (with transfer of public land for cession-of-use housing cooperative initiatives), as can be seen in the following press reports: http://eldigital.barcelona.cat/nou-concurs-public-per-impulsar-el-cohabitatge_347663.html; http://eldigital.barcelona.cat/vols-ser-cooperativista-i-construir-el-teu-habitatge_397617.html; and http://ajuntament.barcelona.cat/noubarris/ca/noticia/barcelona-traurza-a-concurs-pzblic-sis-solars-municipals-per-impulsar-el-cohabitatge.

ing cooperatives in these countries occupy notable quantitative importance within the whole stock of dwellings (Etxebizitzako Behatokia-Observatorio Vasco de la Vivienda 2012).[161]

Thus, in Denmark, for example, 125,000 dwellings are managed under the Andel model, and they are particularly prevalent in Danish cities. In Germany, the importance of housing cooperatives within the constructed housing stock is very significant and the right to use scheme is dominant, meaning that nearly five million people reside in housing cooperatives (approximately 6 percent of the German population). In Sweden, the National Federation of Swedish Co-operatives, HSB (Hyresgästernas sparkasse - och byggnadsförening, Savings and Construction Association of the Tenants), manages around 400,000 dwellings, most of which (310,000) correspond to the model equivalent to cession of use whereby the residents are tenants and the property remains within the cooperative.

Various countries in Northern Europe, then, have made much use of this formula (Merino 2012; Etxezarreta and Merino 2013), but a long tradition also exists on other continents, in countries that include Uruguay (Ghilardi 2016) and Quebec (Bouchard 2005). Similarly, in Manhattan, New York, there is the Cooperative Village, a cooperative development that was in operation from 1930 to 1956, comprising four cooperatives and 4,500 apartments in twelve buildings.[162]

In Spain, to date, although we already mentioned that the legislation does make such experiences possible, only very few have materialized, and that is why they have fallen under the category of *social innovation* in this territory (Etxezarreta et al. 2015).

---

161 As a middle path between a tenant cooperative and one that is geared toward ownership, the shared ownership model is being implemented in Ireland, which might prove of interest to collectives wishing to have access to property but without sufficient means to do so. Via this system, members on an individual basis and the cooperative as a collective acquire 50 percent ownership of the properties, favoring access to 50 percent individual funding for each member through mortgages negotiated with banking institutions under preferential conditions (Etxebizitzako Behatokia-Observatorio Vasco de la Vivienda 2012).

162 https://en.m.wikipedia.org/wiki/Cooperative_Village.

Today, however, a growing interest in these subjects can be perceived in various fields.[163] Thus, a recent contribution from a study of social housing provision in Spain (Pareja Eastaway and Sánchez Martínez 2017) points to housing cooperatives, and banks, as a new actor for such provision.

Likewise, another recent study conducted a survey of good housing policy practices at the regional and local level in the European Union (Observatorio de la Realidad Social-Errealitate Sozialaren Behatokia 2016), in which, among other initiatives, cooperative housing experiences in Sweden, England, and Italy, stand out as benchmark housing policies that promote social cohesion.

Meanwhile, there are factors lying outside housing issues that can be included in this interest, such as the powerful problematic of aging in our society and care management, which are issues that induce much debate and interest that affect the fields of psychology, the economy, and gender, among others. In this regard, various research initiatives are underway, providing now (Emakunde 2016) and in the future (the MOVICOMA project, that is, movimento de vivienda colaborativa de personas mayores, the senior citizens' collaborative housing movement) very interesting results that also coincide in many aspects with the approach of the present study.

Lastly, these cooperative housing initiatives under assignment of use often (though not necessarily) involve a cohousing or collaborative housing project. This concept can be analyzed paying attention to different aspects or typologies, and one of the most commonly employed is the age of cooperative members. In this regard, we can distinguish between senior cohousing and intergenerational cohousing. Senior cohousing covers members who are approaching the third age and contemplate a common active project of group living, in which medical installations and adapted living and suchlike tend to be envisaged. The idea is not to reproduce projects in the shape of retirement homes, but to create active group living in which cooperative members may participate in courses, workshops,

---

163 Despite this fact, many researches still concentrate on the traditional dichotomy between renting and owning in housing research (Pareja Eastaway and Sánchez Martínez 2015; Módenes and López-Colas 2012, 2014).

and shared household chores, and benefit by being released from performing the tasks that members decide to outsource, such as cleaning, laundry, and other such chores.

Intergenerational cohousing encompasses various kinds of families, with members of all ages. The projects tend to involve common

Table 9.1.
Panel of interviewed experts and users

	Name	Category: expert/ user	Association/collective
1	**Miguel Ángel Mira**	Expert	Jubilares Association
2	**Nacho García**	User	Entrepatios Cooperative. Intergenerational project, Madrid
3	**Mario Yoldi**	Expert	Basque Government. Ex-Director of Housing Planning and Operational Processes
4	**Ana Lambea**	Expert	Lecturer Complutense University of Madrid, specialty housing cooperative law
5	**Jaime Moreno**	User	Trabensol Cooperative. "Senior", Torremocha de Jarama, Madrid.
6	**Raúl Robert**	Expert	Founding member of Sostre Civic
7	**Leo Bensadón**	Expert	Lógica'eco, Green Cohousing
8	**Borja Izaola**	Expert and user	Sustraiak, habitat design
9	**Daniel López**	Expert	Department of Psychology and Education. Open University of Catalunya

childcare spaces, activity rooms, and so on. This kind of cohousing, even though cohousing experiences were originally intergenerational (Durrett 2015), seems to pose more problems when materialized in some of the initiatives that have recently appeared in the Spanish context,[164] partly because of the great variety of family types and

---

164 Judging by many that have fallen by the wayside: among others, Housekide,

variations in the economic situation of the members. As we see in the next section, the success rate of these projects is appreciably lower than that registered for senior projects.

Summary of Research Results Concerning Emerging Tenant Cooperative Initiatives in Spain

In recent research conducted on emerging tenant housing cooperative initiatives in the Spanish context (Etxezarreta, Cano, and Merino 2016, Etxezarreta et al. 2018), study was devoted to this phenomenon, both qualitatively and through interviews held between January and May 2016. We focused our qualitative analysis on these kinds of housing cooperatives to underscore the innovation required where property type is involved; first, by the cession-of-use cooperative concept, and, second, by the way of living that is coming to the fore in these cooperatives: cohousing, or the rise of collaborative housing. Both ideas represent a change in the manner of understanding housing ownership in Spain, an innovation that, while tentative, has expectations of taking root in different collectives.

All told, nine interviews were held, with experts and users of tenant housing, with a semi-structured script that had the following outline: operationalization block, experience development block, economic and financial block, and architectural block (open, and eco architecture).

The conclusion drawn from this research was that the cohousing phenomenon is being experienced as a new innovative phenomenon in Spain, although it has a long tradition in other countries. These experiences in some cases are flourishing, while in many others they have failed or no longer exist.

As regards successes, the senior cohousing initiatives should be highlighted, as they are thriving the most. And it appears that both they and most people associated with this cooperative area accept the idea that senior cohousing in Spain seems to all effects to be a formula for success (Etxezarreta, Cano, and Merino 2016,

---

Etxekoop (the two initiatives in Euskadi), and so on.

Etxezarreta et al. 2018). Map 1 shows the successful experiences of senior cohousing in Spain: Trabensol, Profuturo, Santa Clara, and so forth.

By contrast, within the developments that have so far occurred, intergenerational experiences have had the lowest success rate, as is the case of Housekide, Etxekoop, and so on, although there are also experiences of success in this area, such as Entrepatios, Laborda, and others. This lower success rate is due to different factors:

- The financial question tends to be one of the most limiting factors, since the job insecurity of young people may act both as an incentive (to seek innovative, more affordable formulas for obtaining accommodation) and as an insuperable obstacle (because they might not reach the minimum requirements demanded by the financing

Map 9.1.
Successful senior cohousing experiences in Spain

bodies, such as the insistence that the monthly payment should not exceed 30–35 percent of family income).

- The cultural, sociological, or anthropological factor that, above all in countries in Southern Europe, has made housing something more than an accommodation service. For most families it constitutes their principal asset, their most important patrimony, and their way of saving for the future and for their descendants. Accordingly, young people from medium-to-high socioeconomic strata do not choose to go down this avenue.

- Administrative difficulties are also shown to be one of the problem areas these cooperatives come up against.

- On the architectural side, there is clearly an interest in making efficient use of the buildings, respecting where possible ecological standards and the environment. Efforts are also made for the buildings to encourage and facilitate group living, with common, open spaces as part of the cooperative itself.

These tenant cooperatives show the new initiatives that, following the crisis in the property sector, are emerging in Spain. These projects place much emphasis on the social (bottom-up) construction of the cooperative to lend the project greater solidity and durability. The new initiatives answer new housing needs that the traditional market cannot cover and, while they are only taking their first steps, they are making powerful headway in Spain. The qualitative approach revealed difficulties in starting up and consolidating projects, points in common in operationalization and functioning, and a greater grasp of the difficulties, especially in intergenerational cooperatives (Etxezarreta, Cano, and Merino 2016, Etxezarreta et al. 2018.

The Institutional Side: Tenant Cooperatives and Public Housing Policies in Euskadi

Over time the Basque government has stood out among autonomous administrations within the Spanish context for taking the most initiatives in terms of pioneering initiatives and good practices in the housing field (Hoekstra, Heras, and Etxezarreta 2010).

Housing expenditure in Euskadi has traditionally been a very small budget item, taking up around 0.8 percent of social spending, while in other countries far higher amounts are allocated to this sector, as can be seen from the figures for France, Germany, and the United Kingdom (2.6 percent, 2.1 percent, and 5.1 percent, respectively). According to Eustat, the Basque Statistics Office, the statistic for social benefit expenditure distribution, by function and by country, places the average for the European Union EU28 (the twenty-eight member states of the EU) spending on housing at 2.1 percent (Eustat 2017).[165]

To summarize the historical outline, Basque government housing policies, starting from practically residual levels, intensified in the late 1990s and the early2000s and resulted in the growing promotion and construction of social housing.

It was at just that historical point when housing cooperatives (in their traditional form) experienced a phase of proliferation, in the 1990s (Etxezarreta and Etxezarreta 2007). That expansion went hand in hand with an increase in social housing, as housing cooperatives served as an instrument for the promotion and construction of dwellings in Spain, offering lower-cost housing to members of those cooperatives.

As noted in the first section of this chapter, housing cooperatives were used as a tool in social housing construction to reduce costs in the housing promotion and construction phases for social sectors that had greater difficulties in gaining access to housing.

The housing market in Euskadi (within the Spanish housing system) could be placed alongside the Mediterranean housing systems in line with the classification made by Judith Allen et al. (2004), which in turn applies the categorization coined by Gøsta

---

165 Eustat (2017), distribution by function and by country of social benefit expenditure (horizontal percentage) for 2014. http://www.eustat.eus/elementos/ele0003500/Gasto_en_Prestaciones_Sociales_por_funciones_y_pais__horizontal/tbl0003524_c.html

Esping-Andersen (2000) to classify European welfare systems: very high levels of home ownership, and very little rented housing or other types of tenure, as well as a high incidence of empty housing (Etxezarreta 2007; Cano et al. 2013).

The Basque institutions, however, launched a variety of initiatives and engaged in a process of reflection addressed to discern new formulas that would cover Euskadi's housing needs, paying special attention to other European housing systems in the Scandinavian and continental countries (Denmark, Sweden, Germany, and other European references were studied).[166]

Flowing from these innovative initiatives set in motion by the Basque government, and with the property bubble created in the preceding cycle in full expansion, a series of reports were commissioned, and considerations drawn from them, taking concrete shape later in the Basque Housing Law of 2015. This law was adopted after years of negotiation and various draft bills, and the Basque government brought in, alongside this legislation, the individual right to housing within the Autonomous Community of Euskadi. This law specifically introduces the Andel model concept and its promotion, in the third additional provision, in which the text states:

> Promotion or acquisition of residential blocks by nonprofit associations, under cession of use:
>
> 1. Without prejudice to other forms of self-promotion or promotion through cooperatives or other types of association for purposes of the award of dwellings and annexes to their members, nonprofit private associations setup for the purpose will be able to promote or acquire a block of housing, as a single property, to satisfy the residential needs of their associates, under cession of use.[167]

The Basque legal framework, therefore, expressly reflected the new format, intended to incorporate this different *European* housing

---

166 An institutional trip was made in 2008 to various European countries in which the different systems of tenure were observed (and in which the profile of the Andel system and tenant cooperatives stood out).

167 *Boletín Oficial del País Vasco* (BOPV, Official Basque Country Gazette) 119, June 26, 2015, 63.

cooperative model within the Basque context, denominating it in Basque Housing Law as the Andel model (June 2015, against which the Spanish government raised an objection of unconstitutionality).[168]

Likewise, this formula was gradually built into the Basque government's Master Housing Plans, beginning with the Master Housing Plan 2010–13, which includes a pilot test conducted for Tenant Cooperatives (TCs).

In parallel, administrative specifications were prepared to regulate cession of use in 2010; the Basque Country was, therefore, legally and administratively prepared to welcome this new TC housing model. However, the research conducted on TCs concluded (Etxezarreta, Cano, and Merino 2016) that, while an occasional attempt at implementing an Andel model scheme had been made, no headway had been made to date on this track.

Notwithstanding, a new institutional avenue has recently been opened, with specific actions that not only enable but effectively promote its application, as is the case announced in Txomin Enea in Donostia. This first action includes the acquisition of a site[169] (in Txomin Enea, Donostia) and its award to a nonprofit association under cession of use.

Qualitatively, this marks a very important difference in the recent history of public housing policies in Euskadi and it is also built in as an area to be developed in the 2018–2020 Master Housing Plan. Concretely, in the process of generating the New Master Housing Plan 2018–2020, the importance afforded to tenant cooperatives is quite evident, as manifested by the new housing access formulas,

---

168 The Constitutional Court (CT) admitted an application to proceed with an appeal from the central government against the Basque Housing Law because it introduced the temporary expropriation of apartments held by banks, among other steps, and it suspended this legislation as a cautionary measure pending their decision as to whether or not this was in line with the Spanish Constitution. "El Constitucional suspende la Ley de Vivienda vasca que permite expropiar," *El País*, April 15, 2016, at http://politica.elpais.com/politica/2016/04/15/actualidad/1460728003_855913.html.

169 Ibai Maruri Bilbao, "Etxebizitza kooperatiben eredua probatuko du Jaurlaritzak," *Berria*, November 24, 2017, at https://www.berria.eus/paperekoa/1857/013/001/2017-11-24/etxebizitza_kooperatiben_eredua_probatuko_du_jaurlaritzak.htm.

especially as a new model aimed at young people (in the seminars organized by the Basque Housing Observatory on November 23, 2017).[170]

Conclusion

Housing cooperatives form part of the social economy, and although in Euskadi this segment of the social economy has not traditionally been so strongly rooted as others are, it witnessed a period of growth in the 1990s, linked to the rise in social housing. The traditional housing cooperatives, meanwhile, once their function of building and awarding homes was completed, disappeared.

In consequence, the contribution of this formula for cooperativism to the criteria and values of the social economy is rather limited (Etxezarreta and Merino 2013). Indeed, although there are many kinds of cooperatives in the housing field, only tenant cooperatives meet social economy criteria in this area, as the other types of housing cooperatives are purely transitory instruments for saving the cost of paying intermediaries.

This legal formula for tenant cooperatives is also closely bound up with another concept in its application: cohousing, or a community living project. Various initiatives of this kind have in fact arisen in the Spanish context (while in Euskadi there have certainly been various failed attempts) and have been studied in recent research (Etxezarreta, Cano, and Merino 2016, Etxezarreta et al. 2018), concluding that tenant cooperatives and senior cohousing are concepts

---

170 In the seminars for the drawing up of the Master Housing Plan 2018–2020, held on November 23, 2017 in Bilbao, a special space was set aside for dealing with this subject, as a third thrust or axis that must be incorporated in the Basque Master Plan, analyzing new formulas of access to housing. This roundtable saw participation from the President of the Basque Youth Council, members of Egunsentia Aurora, speaking of the potential that exists for developing tenant cooperatives and guiding ideas for achieving that, and a member of Green Cohousing, providing similar arguments for the development of cohousing formulas. See http://www.garraioak.ejgv.euskadi.eus/r41-ovad05/es/contenidos/evento/ovv_jornada17/es_ovv_admi/ovv_a_j.html.

that fit together well, and appear to be here to stay. Many factors favor this alternative way of approaching the last phase of the life cycle of many people (active aging, and the issue of healthcare focused from a gender perspective, among other things).

Nonetheless, intergenerational cohousing or, to put it another way, tenant cooperatives as a new way for young people and young families to gain access to housing, are encountering major difficulties. Problems of a financial and cultural nature, and obstacles to finding land where these collective projects can be materialized, frequently do not encourage the success of these initiatives.

In the recent past, however, there has been an important refocusing of housing cooperatives coupled with a redefinition of public housing policies in Euskadi. There is evidence to show a new resurgence of the latter in the Basque Country, and these newly-coined policies go hand in hand with a formula that is not new but *is* innovative in the Basque setting: tenant cooperatives. While successful schemes have received wide publicity at an international level (in Denmark, Quebec, and Uruguay, among other places), in the Basque context such housing cooperatives have not spread significantly until now.

The Basque Housing Law of 2015 introduced the concept of tenant cooperatives, and in the third additional provision of this law the promotion and acquisition of residential blocks by nonprofit associations under cession of use was included. Although at that time certain administrative specifications were made available to those associations who wished to make such requests, it was at the end of 2017 when the first specific action for the acquisition of a plot of land[171] (in Txomin Enea, Donostia) and its allocation to a nonprofit association under a transfer of use agreement was taken.

The real reach of this political initiative to encourage such access to housing can be observed throughout the development of the previously mentioned Master Housing Plan for 2018–2020, which invests this legal formula for housing cooperatives with great importance, facilitating and promoting its implementation and con-

---

171 Maruri Bilbao, "Etxebizitza kooperatiben eredua probatuko du Jaurlaritzak."

solidation. A very significant qualitative change would, therefore, seem to be occurring, with a shift from the minority and sporadic appearance of such projects in Euskadi and Spain stemming from initiatives among some alternative sectors of active citizens who are generally socially and politically committed (as in the cases of Entrepatios, Trabensol, and other steps taken in the Spanish context), to the concretization of a formula that might acquire the status of a public housing policy in Euskadi, following specific institutional actions adopted to promote housing cooperatives.

Bibliography

Allen, Judith, James Barlow, Jesús Leal, Thomas Maloutas, and Liliana Padovani. 2004. *Housing and Welfare in Southern Europe*. London: Blackwell Publishing.

Bouchard, Marie J. 2005. "De l'expérimentation à l'institutionnalisation positive, l'innoovation sociale dans le logement communautaire au Québec." Collection Etudes theoriques no. ET0511. Québec: CRISES.

Cano, Gala, Aitziber Etxezarreta, Kees Dol, and Joris Hoekstra. 2013. "From Housing Bubble to Repossessions: Spain Compared to Other West European Countries." *Housing Studies* 28, no. 8: 1197–1217.

Durrett, Charles. 2015. *El Manual del Senior Cohousing. Autonomía personal a través de la comunidad*. Translated by Asociación Jubilares. Madrid: Dykinson.

Emakunde. 2016. *Arquitecturas del Cuidado. Viviendas colaborativas para personas mayores. Un acercamiento al contexto vasco y a las realidades europeas*. Vitoria-Gasteiz: Emakunde, Instituto Vasco de la mujer.

Esping-Andersen, Gøsta. 2000. *Fundamentos sociales de las economías postindustriales*. Barcelona: Ariel.

Etxezarreta, Aitziber. 2007. "EAEko etxebizitza sistema eta politika Europako testuinguruan." PhD diss. University of the Basque Country.

Etxezarreta, Aitziber, and Enekoitz Etxezarreta. 2007. "EAEko etxe-bizitza-kooperatibak: argi eta ilunak." *Revista Vasca de Economía Social* 3: 145–62.

Etxezarreta, Aitziber, and Santiago Merino. 2013. "Las cooperativas de vivienda como alternativa al problema de la vivienda en la actual crisis económica." *REVESCO: Revista de Estudios Coop-erativos* 113: 92–119.

Etxezarreta, Aitziber, Joris Hokstra, Gala Cano, Estrella Cruz, and Kees Dol. 2015. "Social Innovation and Social Economy: A New Framework in the Spanish Housing Context." Paper presented at the ENHR (European Network for Housing Research) conference in Lisbon, June 29–July 1.

Etxezarreta, Aitziber, Gala Cano, and Santiago Merino. 2016. "Las cooperativas de cesión de uso y el cohousing en España." Paper presented at the CIRIEC-España conference, Valencia, October 19–21.

Etxezarreta, Aitziber, Santiago Merino, Gala Cano, Kees Dol, and Jo-ris Hoekstra. 2018. "The Emergence of Housing Cooperatives in Spain." In *Affordable Housing Governance and Finance in Europe: Innovations, New Partnerships and Comparative Perspectives*, edited by Gerard Van Bortel, Vincent Gruis, Joost Nieuwenhuijzen, and Ben Pluijmers. Oxford: Routledge, Taylor & Francis.

Etxebizitzako Behatokia-Observatorio Vasco de la Vivienda. 2012. *La política de vivienda y las cooperativas de vivienda en Europa.* Vitoria-Gasteiz: Etxebizitzako Behatokia-Observatorio Vasco de la Vivienda.

———. 2015. *Informe sobre las cooperativas y la promoción de VPP.* Vitoria-Gasteiz: Etxebizitzako Behatokia-Observatorio Vasco de la Vivienda.

Fajardo, Gemma. 2013. "Respuestas cooperativas a necesidades de alo-
jamiento." Paper presented at the 7th Meeting on Cooperative
Housing, Universidad Jaume I de Castellón, Valencia, April 15.

Ghilardi, Flávio. 2016. "El cooperativismo de vivienda en Uruguay
y Brasil como parte integrante de la economía social." Paper
presented at the CIRIEC-España conference, Valencia, October 19–21.

Hoekstra, Joris, Iñaki Heras, and Aitziber Etxezarreta. 2010. "Recent
Changes in Spanish Housing Policies: Subsidized Owner-oc-
cupancy Dwellings as a New Tenure Sector?" *Journal of Housing
and the Built Environment* 25, no. 1: 125–38.

Merino, Santiago. 2012. "La cooperativa de viviendas como adminis-
tradora de bienes comunes." Paper presented at the 7th Rule-
scoop International Conference, Valencia, September 5–7.

Módenes, Juan A., and Julián Lopez-Colas. 2012. "El sistema residen-
cial: un esquema conceptual para entender la relación dinámi-
ca entre población y vivienda en España." *Papers de Demografía*
400: 1–30.

———. 2014. "Recent Demographic Change and Housing in Spain:
Towards a New Housing System?" *Revista española de investigaciones sociologicas* 148: 103–34.

Observatorio de la Realidad Social-Errealitate Sozialaren Behatokia.
2016. *Prospección de buenas prácticas en políticas de vivienda en el
ámbito regional y local de la Unión Europea*. Iruña-Pamplona: Gobierno de Navarra, Ikei.

Otxoa-Errarte, Rosa. 2016. "Reforma del régimen de las cooperativas
de viviendas en Euskadi: de la promoción especulativa encubi-
erta a la cooperativa con cesión de uso." Paper presented at the
CIRIEC-España conference, Valencia, October 19–21.

Pareja Eastaway, Montserrat, and María Teresa Sánchez Martínez.
2015. "El retorno del alquiler en España." *Temas para el debate*
252: 44–46.

————. 2017. "More Social Housing? A Critical Analysis of Social Housing Provision in Spain." *Critical Housing Analysis* 4, no. 1: 124–31.

Salinas, Francisco, and Juan José Sanz. 2003. *Las cooperativas de viviendas en España. Desafíos de presente y futuro.* Ávila: Publicaciones Universidad Católica de Ávila.

www.ingramcontent.com/pod-product-compliance
Lightning Source LLC
Chambersburg PA
CBHW031154270326
41931CB00006B/267